AF248545

YUDA MOLK

COMMON SENSE

about

ABORTION

A complete logical analysis of the abortion issue.

Common Sense Press
Washington D.C.

Printed in the United States of America

Library of Congress Catalog Card number 92-090451

ISBN 0-9633910-5-4

Published by: Common Sense Press
1801 Clydesdale Pl. NW #413
Washington DC 20009
Tel (202) 232-8331

Distribution: Order directly from the publisher
or through national distributors

The paper used in this publication meets the minimum
requirements of the American National Standard for
Information Sciences—Permanence of Paper for
Printed Library Materials, ANSI Z39.48-1984.

1 2 3 4 5 6 7 8 9 (Current printing first digit)

*This book is dedicated to all people who express their humanness by making intelligent life choices. In particular to my mother who chose **not** to abort me. My eternal bodiless soul (namely, the poor would-be or unmaterialized me) would have forgiven her, though, had she made the alternative choice. Not just my life, but even my "right to life" was won through her will and not merely by conception.*

"A person belongs to himself, not to others and not to the society as a whole."

—Supreme Court Justice Blackmun in Bowers vs. Hardwick (S. Ct 106 pp 2848).

Disclaimer

What is said about the 'pro-life' in this book refers to the general pro-life philosophy as reflected by and deduced from the actions and rhetoric of people who choose to call themselves pro-life. Although my remarks are not directed against any particular individual or group of individuals, anyone who voluntarily identifies him or herself with the pro-life philosophy takes the risk that my criticism of that philosophy applies to them, a consequence for which the author disclaims any responsibility.

Furthermore, this book only represents the thinking of its author, exercising his right to free thought, and in fact, to free speech, by thinking it aloud. While inviting his readers to share his thoughts, he does not tell them what to do or how to feel, and therefore categorically disclaims any responsibility for any actions taken (or not taken) or any emotion experienced (or not experienced) by them that can be alleged to come as a result of reading this book.

Biographical Note

The author received the degree of Ph.D. in mathematical statistics from George Washington University (1970), and feels he probably deserves no lesser degree from the "University of Life" due to his extensive traveling (137 countries, communicating in 13 languages) and other social experiences. He decided to write this book after being disgusted with the stupidity, prejudice, hypocrisy, and deception that control not only our public lives but, for many of us, even our personal lives. He is convinced that if more people can be persuaded to use common sense beyond their preconditioning, our planet will be a much better place to live in.

This book is not intended to interfere with the subjective private moral judgment of anyone who, due to being conditioned by religion or otherwise, believes that human life begins at conception, and that abortion therefore is morally wrong. But only to the extent that such individuals practice their own beliefs *in private,* that is, *choose not to terminate their own unwanted pregnancies due to their moral convictions.* All I intend to show is that there are equally strong logical arguments for alternative beliefs (to the point that the conception criterion leads to a much stricter criterion, one that the pro-lifers would find impossible to live with). The implication is that *the pro-lifers' belief cannot be imposed on the society at large.* Just as much as a pro-lifer has the right to opt for no abortion according to her belief, a pro-choicer should have the right to opt for an abortion following her own moral convictions. The imposition of the pro-lifers' principle amounts to the imposition of a religion, which is prohibited by the Constitution.*

A democratic society that gives women the right to bear children should also give women the right not to bear them.

Contents

Preface

This book constitutes one chapter of a much more comprehensive book entitled *Common Sense* (yet unpublished), which deals in a systematic logical manner with all aspects of living in society, including morality, sexuality, religion, law, and politics. It first establishes four principles (interests) characterizing a modern progressive democratic society: rationality, quality of life, protection (security), and liberty (autonomy). According to these principles society must act rationally, promote the quality of life of its members, protect them from outside factors, as well as from each other, and ensure their liberty (autonomy). The last two, protection and autonomy, are in conflict of interest since if people are allowed to do as they please, including performing harmful actions, then others are not protected. Thus, society, through the laws it enacts, should provide a proper balance between protection and autonomy, not always an easy task (even more difficult when the protection and the autonomy are related to the same individual, so that society is depriving individuals of autonomy for their own protection).

The issue of abortion is unique in that it involves protection of an entity (the unborn) that is only a potential member of society. The interest of society in protecting such an entity is very much in dispute;

and what makes matters worse is that it can only be done at the expense of society's undisputed interest to ensure autonomy for women. Among the many issues involved in the debate over abortion, morality, in particular its interrelation with legislation, plays a large part. To get into morality in depth and in connection with still other issues, the reader must wait until my complete book is published; however, inasmuch as the abortion issue is concerned, the explanation in the appendix (where Chapter III of Crum's book is discussed) will do. Thus, for all practical purposes, this book is self contained, standing by itself as an independent unit. It is written in a language suitable for the general audience, without compromising its academic quality.

The issue of abortion being as hot as it is, and the confusion about it as overwhelming as it is, I believe this book should be read by all Americans regardless of their opinion about the issue. The readers who are already pro-choice will know even better why; the pro-life will see more clearly what they are up against, and may take advantage of the golden opportunity given them here to revise their thoughts and modify, or at least moderate, their position. And those who have not yet made up their mind, probably will.

Introduction

Since the Vietnam war there has been no single issue dividing the American people so sharply as the issue of abortion. In the eyes of people like myself, who care about people and cherish life, it seems bizarre and incomprehensible that the millions of already existing children in this country (let alone the hundreds of millions in the Third World), who are neglected, hungry, homeless, uneducated, and some even drug addicted, do not seem to attract the attention and receive care from those who call themselves pro-lifers. Instead, such people keep themselves busy protecting fertilized eggs, which would mean adding more children to the list of the suffering. It also grieves me to witness the erosion of the 1973 *Roe vs. Wade* decision by recent unwise Supreme Court rulings that have thrown the abortion issue from the judiciary (where it was so fairly and elegantly solved) back into the political arena, where it can again play havoc. Now all the urgent problems that this country has to tackle — failing economy, foreign takeovers, unemployment, homelessness, drug abuse, crime, deteriorating race relations, to name just a few — must give way to become secondary campaign issues, where candidates are to be judged more and more by their attitudes about the single issue of abortion (and forget about everything else!). It seems that only in America, among all the nations of the world, can so many people — almost all of whom are middle class, economically established (but apparently detached from reality) — afford the luxury of dealing with issues so irrelevant to daily life as what happens inside the wombs of women they don't even know and never cared about. These people calling themselves pro-lifers (aren't we all?) claim in the name of morality (supposedly not necessarily religious), that ovaries become, upon fertilization, full-fledged human beings who deserve to be endowed with the same legal status existing human beings now enjoy, to the extent that aborting them constitutes murder. According to this claim any woman who conceives, even as a result of rape (an egg fertilized by a rapist is obviously as human as any other fertilized egg, even though it may contain some "bad seed" contributed by the genes of the rapist), must carry the fetus to term no matter what (save, perhaps, where continuance of the pregnancy gravely endangers her life). Thus the well-being of already existing human beings (namely women) with already crystallized personalities, aspirations, sensitivities, desires, and moral beliefs, must be sacrificed in order to give a fetal tissue the chance to become human (a chance only, since conception does not always result in a live birth). From the woman's point of view what the pro-lifers wish to impose on her turns out to be:

1) ***Rape*** — as it deprives her of the right to control her own body, forcing her to engage her feminine body parts in activities that she does not favor, which is no different than what the conventional (sexual) rapist does to her.

2) ***Dehumanizing*** — as it converts her into a breeding machine, very much reminiscent of what was done in Nazi Germany.

3) ***Undemocratic*** — as it forces one segment of society to submit to the moral beliefs of another segment that does not even constitute the majority. (This is not to say that even if it did, it would be entitled to impose this particular belief.)

In this book, I intend to show that the case against abortion as it is presented by the pro-lifers is actually a purely religious issue.[1] It is not even based upon the general philosophy of religion or the belief in God, but rather on the adoption of a very specific religious dogma. Furthermore, given the attitude of the pro-lifers regarding one particular case (that of in-vitro fertilization), I will show clearly that when the choice is between human life and dogma, the pro-lifers abandon life, the very thing they claim to be "pro-," and choose to support the dogma instead; hence their true name should be "pro-dogma" rather than "pro-life." From establishing that the pro- lifers' case against

---

[1] No wonder that it is almost exclusively religious groups that are involved in the pro-life movement.

abortion is religious, it follows that imposing this view through legislation would be unconstitutional as it violates the principle of separation of state and church.

But is abortion a pro-life issue at all? And if it is, which one, the life of the woman or the life of the unborn?[2] I will answer this question in the next Chapter.

---

[2] Having an abortion is obviously "pro-" relating to the life of the unwillingly pregnant woman, which is messed up by the unwanted pregnancy!

Chapter I

The Choice Aspect of Abortion

What makes the abortion issue so controversial is that it involves two rights (and "right" should be taken here in both of its meanings): the right of the unborn (to life) and the right of the pregnant woman (to choice). From society's point of view it seems as though some balance has to be struck between the two rights to forge a compromise. "But how can you compromise on murder?" ask the pro-lifers. That makes the argument totally dependent on the determination of the status of the unborn.[1] If it is a human being — and that is why it is so crucial for the pro-lifers to accord it with such status, and for the pro-choicers to deny it same — then it seems that abortion is tantamount to murder.

---

[1] The question of the human status of the unborn will be treated thoroughly in the next chapter, both for the sake of making sure the presentation is complete and comprehensive, exhausting all aspects of the issue, as well as to appease the consciences of many people.

However, this is not so at all. I now intend to show that, contrary to what is believed and held, even if the unborn is considered a full-fledged human being, abortion is not murder; that is, *the status of the unborn is not at all the decisive factor in the issue of abortion.* Thus, even if the pro-lifers succeed in amending the Constitution to include fertilized eggs as "persons," it would do them very little good, if at all, in their fight against abortion. The status of the unborn by itself does not determine what is required of the mother to keep it alive, just as my undisputed human status does not impose any obligation upon my readers to keep me alive at their expense. For example, suppose I threatened suicide if, within a month of its publication, my book were to sell less than five million copies. Would this impose a moral, let alone a legal, duty on all the American people to run to the stores and buy my book? To make my point clear I wish to work through some examples. The issue in all of them is: *How much sacrifice is required of one person to save the life of another?*

Suppose you observe a fire in your neighbor's house, where the parents are absent and a small child is asleep upstairs in the burning house. You could think for yourself that the fire and its consequences are none of your business, not even bothering to call the fire department. I am sure that such a selfish action on your part should and would be considered immoral by consensus, and maybe even illegal. Suppose you did call the fire department but feared that they would not show up in time to save the child, that the child's only chance would be that you personally try to rescue him, at the risk of losing your own life or at least getting badly burned and disfigured. People would regard you as a hero if you were to take that risk, but are you morally, let alone legally, obliged to do so? Obviously, we are morally as well as legally free to chose our own life over the life of another, as one can deduce from the principle of self defense.[2] Hence, you are not required to *sacrifice* your life to save the child, but are you still required *to risk it?* If yes, then what degree of risk should you take? Or, even if there is no risk to your life, and you would only get burned, then are you required to sacrifice that part of your well-being in order to save the life of the child? It is fairly clear that your situation in this case is analogous to that of the pregnant woman who, if abortion is outlawed, would be required by society to make the sacrifice. Now, if you are tempted to dismiss the above analogy because of the physical risk involved (as if pregnancy is not risky), then consider one more example, where risk is not the issue but sacrifice of your quality of life is.

In this second example we have a sick person in the hospital, who needs a transfusion of blood/plasma/bone marrow, whatever, and because of your particular biological qualities (DNA, for example) you are the

---

[2] Granted, there is a difference here to the extent that the term self defense implies an attack by person whose life may be considered worth less than yours because he committed a crime. However as you are not a judge to determine that (that is, you are not authorized to punish him), then before trial, this person's life should equal the life of anybody else; consequently, *the only reason* you are allowed to kill him is that you are allowed to value your life more than the life of other people.

only person known to be able to give this person this particular transfusion. If you refuse, the sick person is sure to die. In order to perform the transfusion you must lie side by side with the sick person connected to him/her by an infusion set for a period of nine months. Can society make you do it? The analogy here is clear: you stand for the pregnant woman, and the sick person stands for the unborn. As a possible argument against the analogy one can claim that there is a difference — since the pregnant woman must act to terminate the pregnancy, whereas here you could simply not agree to connect to the sick person. In other words, your responsibility for his/her death is by omission and not by commission, hence you are "less of a murderer." Well, it is a technical difference only, and the following minor amendment to the example will take care of it.

Suppose that while walking down a back alley you are abducted by the sick person's family and they put you under anesthetic. When you wake up, you find yourself in a hospital bed connected to the sick person by the infusion set. Your refusal to save this person's life would now involve an action on your part: disconnecting the set and getting the hell out of the hospital. Would it then be immoral for you to do it, or would it now be justified for the government (say, in the form of the hospital staff) to force you to remain for nine months infusion-connected to the sick person against your will? One might argue further that conception (of which the analogue is the abduction and forced transfusion to the sick person) is to an extent the woman's fault and could be avoided if she were to refrained from sex.[3] My response to this argument is that the abduction is also to an extent "the fault of the abducted" in that he or she was walking in a back alley, and whoever walks in back alleys takes risks and therefore should not complain of being abducted and connected by an infusion set to sick people in hospitals. The analogy is now complete, and my task of giving readers some more food for thought is now accomplished. From the legal standpoint, there are several precedents in which the courts denied any right of the state to force people to contribute any parts of their biological substance to save other peoples' lives. We can see clearly that the argument raised here in fact renders most arguments regarding the issue redundant, since the status of the unborn (whether it is a "person" or not) becomes irrelevant, and the right of the mother to refuse to be "infusion-connected" to the unborn is deeply entrenched in the law.

Now to dig even deeper into the apparent murderous act perpetrated by a pregnant woman upon having an abortion, consider this. Even though the unborn cannot be accused of any wrong-doing for being in the womb, from the woman's point of view it is not at all an innocent person maliciously

---

[3] Refraining from sex is not the only way to avoid unwanted pregnancy and thus the need to have an abortion. Other ways to accomplish this would be to commit suicide, to live in a bubble, to get sterilized, or to never even speak to anyone of the opposite sex. The truth is that requiring a woman to refrain from sex in order to avoid unwanted pregnancy is just as much an imposition on her quality of life as requiring her to refrain from having an abortion.

attacked by her while quietly minding its own business. It is exactly the other way around. It is the pregnant woman who, while quietly minding her own business, bothering no one, is suddenly attacked by the unborn that not only penetrated her home, her castle, but actually invaded her very body without permission. Suppose it is a grown-up person who breaks into her apartment uninvited and forces his body upon her declaring his intention to continue using her body to satisfy his selfish needs for the next nine months. Would you then say that she should submit rather than free herself from him, even if the only way to do it would be to kill him? Should she be considered a murderess for her act of self-defense?

I ask my readers to note that the woman's act is not an act of punishment, so that the fault (or moral status) of the intruder is irrelevant. For example, if the rapist turns out to be legally insane, and hence criminally innocent, that would not make her act more like homicide. Thus, the fact that the unborn is not responsible for its actions (penetrating her and sticking to her womb) is irrelevant. From the woman's point of view it is not innocent but rather an intruder against whom an act of self-defense is legitimate, regardless of the "moral status" of the intruder. The resulting death of the intruder is only a *side effect* of this legitimate act. Murder has nothing to do with it.

The above argument shows clearly that, in essence, the right to abortion is a natural right, just as self-defense against rapists, refusal to risk one's life to save children trapped in burning houses, or refusal to be connected by infusion sets to sick people in hospitals are. To quote Justice Blackmun from *Bower vs. Hardwick* (S.Ct 106 pp 2848): "a person belongs to himself, not to others and not to the society as a whole." This is the American way of looking at the individual in contrast to the Marxist-Leninist-Stalinist or the Nazi regimes making the individual the property of the state. In our society, the state or any person may not use the body of a woman for any reason, including the satisfaction of the religious and moral convictions of a religious minority with political leverage (and for that matter it could even be a majority). Thus we do not have a conflict between pro-life and anti-life. *We all cherish life.* Many women who went through abortion also raised beautiful children. The conflict is between *pro-choice* and *anti-choice*, and *WHOEVER IS ANTI-CHOICE IS IN FACT ANTI-AMERICAN.*

In spite of what was argued before, we are a little bit in trouble when we get to the very end of pregnancy when the unborn is practically equivalent to a baby. In the framework of our theory we can justify the interference of society in this case to the extent that the additional sacrifice required there of the woman is marginal, which is also consistent with our examples. If all that is required from a person in the first example is a little inconvenience, such as calling the fire department, and he or she refuses, he or she may be blamed. If all he or she needs to do is give half a pint of blood to save an injured person's life, and he or she refuses, he or she may be blamed. And likewise, if the intruder only wants to touch the hair of the woman and then go away and she chooses to kill him rather than let him do it, she may be blamed. The fact that in borderline cases the conclusions differ[4] does not make the case weaker, but rather strengthens it because of the logical consistency. Yet to present a broader picture and offer a backup argument, or simply because the conclusion has been allowed flexibility in the margins, I will continue to investigate the issue from other angles as well. In the next chapter the focus is shifted from the "choice" aspect of abortion to its "life" aspect. However, the reader should bear in mind that due to our presentation here it has very little relevance to the issue.

---

[4] This exception regarding abortion has little practical significance since very few abortions are performed in the late stage of pregnancy.

Chapter II

The Life Aspect of Abortion
(When Does Human Life Begin?)

If we (temporarily) set aside all our arguments regarding choice, then the basic question on which the pro-lifers' case stands, or falls, seems to be, "When does human life begin?" The truth is that the answer to this question is *arbitrary by definition*, since *only after we define human life can we inquire when it begins.* Now, the pro-lifers' supposedly secular definition recognizes as a human being "any living organism that possesses a complete set of human genes." By this definition, the beginning of human life is the point at which this codification occurs, that is, conception. The fact that, apart from containing the genetic code, the fertilized egg is no more than a piece of tissue consisting of two, four, eight, or more cells (this depends on how long it has been since fertilization), making it equivalent to some of the most inferior biological forms of life, does not concern them. The truth is that the dogma "life begins at conception" existed way before humanity knew about the existence of genes. The definition was chosen to conveniently fit the dogma. If "codification" is the magic word, then the pro-lifers marked their target after shooting the arrow. Obviously, just as the pro-lifers choose to view conception as the cut-off point, others are free to choose any other criterion that makes sense.

For example, one may choose to be more lenient than the pro-lifers and regard the formation of the human brain as the starting point of human life,[1] on the premise that it is the human brain that makes us superior to other living things. Or, one may stick with viability, the criterion used by the Supreme Court in *Roe vs. Wade.* Viability refers to the ability of the fetus to breath by itself if detached from the womb of its would-be mother. Since both the formation of the brain as well as viability occur between the sixth and the seventh months of pregnancy, then, by these criteria, a less than six-month-old fetus is not a human being.

On the other hand, one may choose to be more strict than the pro-lifers. Let's call the fertilized egg containing the complete set of genes a "full-gener", and the unfertilized egg, as well as the sperm, each containing only half of the genes, a "half-gener". By the pro-lifers' criterion then a full-gener, or "everything that contains a complete set of human genes," is a human being. Why not be more "compassionate"

---

[1] Remember, we deal here only with "human life." Even the pro-lifers do not require society to protect all forms of life, including animals.

and define as human "everything that contains human genes in whole or in part," which would include half-geners? Objectively, this definition is just as legitimate as the one the pro-lifers adopt, and it implies that not only the destruction of the fertilized egg, but also the destruction of the unfertilized egg and the sperm, constitutes murder.

The bottom line is that the establishment of a criterion for the beginning of human life is arbitrary and relative, once we look for it in the pre-birth realm. To shed more light on the criterion of conception or the full-gener criterion, I must elaborate some more on the half-gener criterion that was introduced above to include unfertilized eggs and sperm as humans. In fact, I will show by logical deduction — with intellectual honesty being the only prerequisite — that *the adoption of the first criterion must lead to adoption of the second.*

Contraception — Murder "on the Average"

It is not unreasonable to assume that a fertile woman having normal sex and not practicing birth control will at some point in her life get pregnant. (Statistically, it is *virtually certain* that this will happen, and more than once.) That means that of all ovulations during her life time, there is one egg, which we'll label E, that becomes fertilized with near certainty.[2] If this woman uses birth control and never gets pregnant, this would-be fertilized egg E is destroyed. Indeed,

---

[2] Remember again that even a fertilized egg is not certain to become a baby.

we cannot identify this egg "Personally" (individually), or say how many such eggs are wasted through the use of contraceptives, but we can say this much: *By using contraceptives, every healthy, fertile woman destroys in a long run ("on the average"), at least one egg that would otherwise have been fertilized.*

Now what is the difference between contraception and abortion? Well, in both cases fertilized eggs are destroyed, except that in the former case it is done *"on the average,"* whereas in the latter, it is done *in actuality.* Using the pro-lifer's terminology, in both cases a murder is committed — except that in the case of abortion the victim is known to us, while in the case of the use of contraceptives, the victim is anonymous. Is it less of a crime to kill an anonymous person than to kill a specific person? Well, let us take a real-life example, which occurred in Israel in the early 1980s. There was a demonstration attracting a huge crowd, and an opponent of the demonstrators shot blindly (randomly) into the crowd and killed one of the demonstrators. Even though he did not aim to kill this particular individual, he was found guilty of murder (where "intention" is an element of the charge). The fact that the identity of the victim was unknown to him when he shot into the crowd does not make his crime less forgivable than if he had approached this particular individual and shot him at point-blank range. The difference between killing a specific fertilized egg, and consistently killing sperm or eggs and thus, in the long run, killing an anonymous (otherwise living) fertilized egg, is exactly the same as the difference between shooting to kill from point-blank range and doing the same in a random manner. The bottom line is that there is no moral ground to forbid destruction of fertilized eggs while allowing the destruction of sperm or unfertilized eggs. In other words, in the terminology I previously introduced, *half-geners deserve just as much protection as full-geners (the pragmatic consequence of their destruction being the same).*

Contraception — Genocide "by Probability"

The argument in favor of preserving half-geners (sperm) can even go beyond the one just introduced. It can be justifiably argued that destruction of sperm is even *more severe* than destruction of fertilized eggs, just as genocide is more severe than simple murder. For that purpose I would like to introduce a concept I label *"murder by probability."* To understand this concept, think of the following (Russian roulette) example. Suppose a person, call him A, loads a pistol with one real bullet and five blanks. He then spins the cartridge, aims at person B, and then pulls the trigger. This action does not indicate an obvious intention to kill, because the action would result in killing only one sixth of the time in the long run. By pulling the trigger the gunman (A) only indicated "an intention to kill with a 1/6 (16.7%) probability." Now if the action of pulling the trigger did in actuality lead to killing (that is, the game of Russian roulette resulted in shooting the real bullet rather than a blank), then A is guilty of ***"murder by 1 / 6 (16.7%) probability."*** Yet the court would consider him a (full-fledged) murderer. This shows clearly that "murder by probability" is treated as severely as "murder." It may be true that if the probability were smaller, we would have the tendency to see it more leniently, but obviously our leniency would only be slight and by no means proportional to the probability. If the punishment for murder is 24 years in jail, then "murder by 1/6 probability" may be somewhat less severely punished, but by no means by only 4 years — one sixth of the punishment for murder. Now, suppose that with the pulling of the trigger a blank was shot and no harm was done to person B. My understanding is that under those circumstances person A would still be guilty of attempted murder (even though what he was actually doing was only "attempting murder by 1/6 (16.7%) probability." The fact that Mr Chance was nice to B, saving him from death by choosing a blank, should not constitute a good enough reason to absolve A of his malicious act that could have resulted in B's death. The only consideration A gets in this case is that he is charged with a lesser crime (attempted murder in lieu of murder).

We can summarize the concept of "murder (including attempted murder) by probability" as "an action that intends — with some probability of success — to kill a human being." In the "Russian roulette" example, the victim was human for sure but the weapon had only a 1/6 probability of doing the job. "Murder by 1/6 probability" could also be accomplished differently. Suppose you intend to kill a person and your pistol is loaded with one bullet. When you arrive at the spot from which you intend to shoot and you look down to the prospective victim's garden where you expect him to be, you see not one, but six figures. Five are dummies and one is your intended victim, but you cannot tell which is which. You aim and shoot at one of the figures. In this case, the weapon is sure to be effective but the object has only 1/6 probability of being human.

Now that we understand what is meant by "murder (including attempted murder) by probability" we can apply it to our case. Upon ejaculation during sexual intercourse, many millions of sperm enter the vagina. Each of these organisms has a certain probability, however small, of fertilizing an egg (or becoming human in the pro-lifers' lingo). If contraceptives are used to destroy sperm (say sperm-killing cream) then a "murder by probability" is committed. The destruction of a whole batch of as many as half a billion sperm amounts to "genocide by probability" ("murder by probability of a population big enough to inhabit a continent"). Such genocide, albeit "by probability" only, occurring as a result of the use of sperm-killing cream, should be considered more severe than the murder of one single individual, something that supposedly occurs when an abortion is performed. Thus, it is more of a crime to use sperm-killing contraceptives than it is to perform an abortion.

The Abortion-Equivalent Star Wars Contraceptive (SWC)

In the last two sections I went into detailed arguments to show the relativity of the conception criterion, which too many people take for granted. I claimed that since we regard "murder on the average" as well as "murder by probability" as murder (and incidentally, the destruction of a fertilized egg is also only a "murder by probability," as it has only a probability of maturing into a full- fledged human), then if the destruction of the fertilized egg is to be considered murder, so should the destruction of the unfertilized egg or the sperm (the last may even be considered genocide). The pro-lifers may still not be convinced and may still stick to their dogma, saying that it is the identifiability of the destroyed object that is the relevant factor (which translates into saying that murder "by probability" as well as murder "on the average" are pardonable). To argue against that let us now assume that there exists an advanced contraceptive, which I now name "the Star Wars Contraceptive" (in short SWC). The effect of the SWC is to kill the sperm once it is in a position at which it is certain that it will make contact with the egg. For instance this device could consist of infinitely small bodies sitting on the periphery of the egg and killing the sperm upon its contact with the egg. The sperm would hit the egg, but would be prevented from penetrating it to cause fertilization. We are now confronted with a situation where

(1) The full genes of the individual to be formed are known to us, because the identity of the would-be-fertilizing sperm is known to us.

(2) The SWC is the one and only reason that fertilization did not occur.

Pragmatically speaking, the effects of an immediate abortion of the fertilized egg and of the use of SWC are identical: in both cases a fully codified potential human being (for the pro-lifers "a human being") is destroyed. It would make no sense whatsoever to cry "murder" in the former case, and approve of the latter. Thus, in the name of common sense, intellectual honesty, and regard for human life, the pro-lifers must hold that the use of such a contraceptive is also murder. But once they do that, they admit that human life begins even before and without conception, which contradicts their dogma that "human life begins at conception."

One may argue that a Star Wars type of contraceptive does not exist and my argument is non-realistic. My answer to this is, first, that I can't rule out the possibility that it does exist, and at any rate given the techniques modern science now have we are not talking science fiction; and second, if the dogma depends on technology, holding true only so long as science has not reached the advanced technology of a Star Wars Contraceptive, then the dogma is not absolute as a dogma should be and hence it is worthless. In addition, suppose you disapprove of a contraceptive that prevents the 100% sure uniting of a given sperm with the egg, then what if it is only 99% or 95% or 90% or even 50%? Where do you set the limit? The conclusion therefore is that the same principle that regards codification of human life as human life, which is the pro-lifers' case against abortion, could present just as good a case against contraceptives as against abortion, and that *the dogma "human life begins at conception" is quite relative, as there is no specific convincing reason why it should be preferred over any other criterion for the beginning of human life.*

The Ultimate Pro-lifers

In the light of the relativity of the pro-lifers' criterion, which is no longer entitled to monopolizing our thinking about human life, it is now high time to start using the right terminology. It is said that if something looks like a duck, walks like a duck, and quacks like a duck —it is a duck. If it walks somewhat differently, it may still be a lame duck. If it does not quack, it may be a dumb duck. However, if it does not look like a duck, does not walk like a duck, and does not quack like a duck — *it is NOT a duck.* A fertilized egg, at least in the first few weeks following fertilization, looks, at most, more like a worm than like a human being, it does not walk or talk, or think like a human being, and in fact, has practically *none of the characteristics of a human being,* except that it contains the blue-print in the form of the genetic code. Is it really legitimate to call this piece of tissue a "human being"? To answer this question we need an example. Suppose — and with generic engineering as advanced as it is today we are not talking science fiction — it would be possible to inject an apple with the DNA cells of an orange, so that slowly but surely during several (say, nine) months these cells act as cancer cells and destroy and replace the apple cells, thus converting it into an orange. It would be completely appropriate to call this fruit an orange at the end of the process, but would it be appropriate to call it "an orange" upon the injection of the orange cells? I refuse to believe that any intellectually honest person would answer this question positively. The right name to call it then would be "an apple with the potential to become an orange." Or if your interest is limited to the "orangeness" of this fruit, call it simply a "potential orange."

Now, anyone who can tell apples from oranges should be able to tell fertilized eggs from human beings. The fertilized egg is NOT a human being. It does not look, walk, or talk like one. What it is, is [a fertilized egg, which means] *an egg that is fertilized,* or an egg that has the *potential* of becoming a human being. If we want to restrict ourselves to language comprising solely the concept "human being," we can call it legitimately *a potential human being* or in short *a "potential human."*[3] But once we speak in terms

---

[3] The appendix, as a part of the discussion of Chapter IV of Crum's book, gives another very convincing reason why the unborn is only a "potential human."

of potential humans, then surely the unfertilized egg and the sperm also become potential humans. In fact, as we have shown, a batch of sperm being ejaculated at the end of just one instance of sexual intercourse is a collection of potential humans big enough to inhabit a continent, or a *potential continental population.* Now, in the right terminology just introduced, what the pro-lifers want is not only the protection of human lives, but also the protection of some potential human lives. They require the society to endow potential humans, in the form of fertilized eggs, with the same right of protection that full-fledged humans now enjoy. Now I ask: if this is so, then why stop at the fertilized eggs? why not go beyond fertilization, giving the same protection to the unfertilized egg and the sperm, which are also potential humans? In other words, if we are to preserve potential human life, then not only abortion is to be prohibited but also all means of birth control and even masturbation. *Moreover, we should be obligated to have sex continually, because every time we are practically able to have sex and choose to abstain, we prevent potential humans from materializing into humans, hence — to use the language of the pro-lifers — we commit murder.*

> SO MY DEAR DEAR PRO-LIFER FRIENDS. PLEASE BEWARE!
> IF YOU CONTINUE YOUR HYPOCRITICAL RELIGIOUS PRACTICE OF
> ABSTENTION, YOU ARE GOING TO BURN IN HELL FOR THE CRIME OF
> MASS MURDER. YOUR ONLY WAY TO AVOID THIS CRUEL PUNISHMENT
> (LASTING FOR THE DURATION OF YOUR WHOLE AFTER-LIFE) IS TO
> GET TO WORK AND *SCREW,SCREW, SCREW!* (EVERY PLACE, ALL THE
> TIME AND AS MANY SEX PARTNERS AS FEASIBLE).

At this point I ask my readers not to be confused by my humor. The truth is that, if one is fanatic enough and consistent enough in one's compulsion for preserving potential humans, then one must reach such an extreme conviction obligating mankind to "screw to the last breath." The philosophy based on this conviction ought to be called *ultimate pro-life* and its adherents — *ultimate pro-lifers.* If the pro-lifers now say that the ultimate pro-lifers' approach is way too extreme, I would answer them that *as ridiculous and extreme as this seems to them, so their requirement for the preservation of fertilized eggs seems to me.* Their cut-off point in the protection of potential human life is no less arbitrary and subjective than the ultimate pro-lifers', and should not be imposed on others, just as the ultimate pro-lifer's more extreme views should not be imposed on them, requiring them and everybody else to engage, willingly or not, in perpetual sexual activity for procreative purposes.

Moreover, since the arguments we presented in each of the last three sections (Murder on the Average, Murder by Probability, and the Star Wars Contraceptive) all concluded that if fertilized eggs should be protected, so should unfertilized eggs and sperm, it follows that an intellectually honest pro-lifer faces a hard dilemma: He must either renounce the dogma or principle he adheres to (that fertilized eggs are protection-deserving humans) or else must become an ultimate pro-lifer.

The Pro-lifers' Public Relations Deception

Now let us analyze the public relations aspect of the pro-lifer's activity, to show that it either indicates absolute ignorance on their part, or constitutes demagoguery, which takes advantage of lack of sophistication on the part of whoever goes for it. They start with the principle (or if you like, postulate or axiom) of the SANCTITY OF HUMAN LIFE, which I will call by its initials "the SHL principle." I am not very happy with the term "Sanctity" due to its religious connotations, and prefer to use a term such as "supervaluability" instead (if there isn't yet such a word in the English language, I am hereby "inventing" it *ad hoc*). However, I would, for simplicity, continue to use the term SHL and ask the reader to understand it in its secular connotation (where S can stand for supervaluability). Now, the SHL principle is accepted by the society at large (save for some criminals) by consensus, so that it is okay to regard it as an axiom. After reminding us of the SHL principle, the pro-lifers proceed to claim that the fertilized egg constitutes human life. Then, applying the SHL principle to the now-declared-human fertilized egg, they deduce that [due to the SHL principle] the fertilized egg must be protected. This constitutes a correct logical (mathematical) procedure *save for one simple thing:* The SHL principle is accepted by all of us as an axiom *only on the premise that it refers to conventional humans,* that is, existing humans having conventional human characteristics, or "persons" as they are referred to by the Constitution. Now, it was just previously established that fertilized eggs are *not humans* (and obviously not by consensus), only *potential humans.* It is indeed only a matter of semantics (however misleading) when the pro-lifers broaden the definition of "humans" to include also "potential (coming-in-the-shape-of-a-fertilized-egg) humans". The problem starts when they take a principle (SHL) accepted by consensus for humans in the narrow (conventional) sense (namely, accepted in the realm of existing human beings) and apply it automatically within the realm of the "broadened humans." How can one expect everything that is true in the old realm to automatically hold true in the new realm?

In mathematics we engage a lot in broadening definitions of concepts, but once we do it, we bother to check all the theorems and see which remain true, and which are rendered false (inapplicable) in the broader realm. Because of the crucial logical step that is missing in the "case against abortion" as presented by the pro-lifers, I feel obligated to bring up an example. I chose a simple one that can be understood by all readers with no more than an elementary school education. We start with the concept of "rectangles." A rectangle can be defined as "a four-sided polygon where the angle between adjacent sides is 90° (right) and opposite sides are equal in length." For rectangles two theorems are true:

Theorem I: The circumference equals twice the sum of any adjacent sides.

Theorem II: The area equals the product of any adjacent sides.

Now let us broaden the definition of "rectangles" to the new concept of "(generalized) rectangles." We define a "(generalized) rectangle" by omitting the requirement that the angle between adjacent sides be a right angle but leaving all the rest intact. Namely, a generalized rectangle is defined as a "four-sided polygon having opposite sides that are equal in length". Actually, our newly defined rectangles are nothing but parallelograms. We can even think of the non-right-angled parallelograms as "potential rectangles" to the extent that upon the "righting" of their angles they become rectangles in the usual sense. Thus our generalized rectangles are either (conventional) rectangles (i.e. right-angled parallelograms), or their potentials (non-right-angled parallelograms), just like generalized or broadened humans are either (conventional) humans or their potentials (unborns). We can easily see that for generalized rectangles Theorem I remains true, but Theorem II is, in general, false: the area of a generalized rectangle no longer equals the product of adjacent sides but rather the products of any side with its distance (i.e., the length of the perpendicular) from the opposite side,[4] the distance being equal to the adjacent side if, and only if, the angle is 90°. In other words, only for those (generalized) rectangles that are also rectangles in the narrower conventional sense will this hold true.

Getting back to the subject now in the light of our example we can depict the analogy as follows:[5] we see that the pro-lifers start with the SHL principle (in the example, Theorem II, that is, the equality of the area to the product of adjacent sides), which is accepted for existing humans (in the example, rectangles in the conventional sense, that is, with right angles). Then they broaden the concept of human life to include potential human life (in the example, broaden the concept of rectangles to also include potential rectangles, namely, non-right-angled parallelograms). Now the pro-lifers apply the SHL principle to the broadened concept of "human life," namely also to "potential human life" (in the example, apply Theorem II to the broader concept of rectangles, to include potential rectangles, i.e., non-right-angled

---

[4] Or equivalently, put in trigonometrical language, in order to calculate this area one has to multiply the product of the adjacent sides by an additional factor: the sine of the angle between them.
[5] See the analogy table next page.

parallelograms) to deduce that "potential humans" (in the form of fertilized eggs) are to be protected (in the example, to deduce that Theorem II holds also for parallelograms, that is, that the area of the parallelogram equals the product of its adjacent sides). Now as we know Theorem II is generally false for parallelograms, we also know by analogy that there is no reason why the SHL principle should be applicable to fertilized eggs. The smoke screen that is used by these pro-life magicians to do the trick

ANALOGY TABLE

REALM	CASE DISCUSSED: HUMANS			ANALOGUE CASE: RECTANGLES		
	description	rule	validity	description	rule	validity
Original	conventional (existing) humans	SHL: human life is sacred	true	conventional (right-angled) rectangles	I: Circomference = (side1 + side2) x 2	true
					II: area = side1 x side2	true
Broadened	broadened (born + unborn) humans	SHL	? (not necessarily true)	broadened (right-angled + non-right-angled) rectangles = parallelograms	I: Circomference = (side1 + side2) x 2	true
					II: area = side1 x side2	false

Conclusion: The SHL principle may still be true in the broader realms, as Theorem I is, but may also be false, as Theorem II is. Thus its validity in the broader realm (of existing + potential humans) cannot be deduced from its validity in the original realm (of existing humans).

is of course the merging of the concept "potential human life" with the concept "actual human life." After the smoke screen is gone, they apply the SHL principle to the new product as if it were the old one. Now, either they are ignorant, or else they believe we are and that they can fool us.

For the benefit of readers who got bored, confused, or simply daunted by the mathematical example here is an easier one. The whole idea of broadening a definition is to find something that the entities conforming to the old definition have in common with those which are added by the new definition. The only thing humans have in common with fertilized eggs is the genetic code. If instead we concentrate on another human property, such as "walking on two legs," then we can broaden the definition of humans by declaring as human "every living thing that walks on two legs." Now our definition includes birds as humans. As long as we remain in the realm of semantics, no harm has been done. However, once we try to apply the SHL principle to the new additions and deduce merely by semantics that the lives of birds are sacred, we engage in deception. Even if we exclude birds from the definition, we remain in trouble, since our definition would still include all animals (such as dogs or bears) trained to walk on two legs, whose lives would become sacred by mere semantics.

To see also from another angle the absurdity resulting from a frivolous transferring/transcending of rules or principles across the lines of their realm of validity, consider this. The pro-lifers' contention amounts to saying that since unborns are potential humans they should be treated as what they potentially are, that is, humans, and that rules applying to humans, such as the SHL, should apply to them as well. Now, humans are mortals, and it is their ultimate destiny to become corpses. Using the pro-lifers' logic, we must apply to humans rules that are valid in the realm of what humans potentially are, (i.e., rules valid in the realm of corpses). It follows that if burning a corpse is not a crime, then neither should burning a human be one. Furthermore, unborns (through the intermediary stage of humans) are potential corpses as well, hence aborting them does not constitute murder.

So When Does Human Life Begin?

We started the chapter with the quest for the beginning of human life. For that end we needed to define "human life," but then it turned out that in our definition we needed to define "human life" in terms of its beginning — a vicious circle. The source of that confusion is no other than that one we encounter when we try to search for the beginning of the universe. People get in trouble when they expect everything to have a beginning. Too many things, especially those that are associated with the existence of the universe and our existence in it do not behave so nicely. ***The right way to look upon the formation of human life is not as an instantaneous act or phenomenon*** (NOW YOU DON'T SEE IT! NOW YOU

*DO!), **but rather as a PROCESS.** This process starts way before conception. The fertilization of the egg is only one stage in this process. The egg by itself is a living organism, but neither before fertilization (with which even the pro-lifers agree) nor after it (with which the pro-lifers would not agree) is it a human being. Neither the egg nor the sperm that fertilizes it comes out of the blue. Both come from humans, themselves the product of the sperm and egg of their parents, and so on and so forth. Where does this chain begin? Well, if you believe science, our ancestors are the apes. But as "ape life" is not "human life," we should search for the beginning of "human life" in the no-man's land (or perhaps in the no-ape's land) of the transition from "ape life" into "human life." This transition, however, was not abrupt, but rather lengthy and gradual (practically "continuous" in mathematical terms). To pick any particular creature in this chain and claim that "this is the first human," namely, that this creature is human, but his parents were apes, is obviously a task no less futile than arbitrary. That leaves the "beginning of human life" as a question mark. Even if we restrict ourselves to analyze only the last nine months of the process, starting with the unfertilized egg (which by consensus is not "human life"), then passing through various intermediate evolutionary stages after fertilization (first resembling an amoeba, later resembling a worm, gaining a tail and then losing it, etc.) and ending with the birth of a baby (by consensus a "human life") we cannot establish any objective criterion to tell us when human life begins. That clearly makes it *a process,* about which all we can say is that it leads to "human life" starting from something less than that. Any criterion whatsoever that anyone would set for the beginning of "human life" somewhere in the midst of this process (such as fertilization, becoming a fetus, being able to breath or think and the like) would be artificial and non-scientific for two reasons:

(1) Different people would favor different criteria (we know, for example, what the pro-lifers think!), and since there is no objective way of resolving this difference, any criterion is subjective and arbitrary.

(2) Suppose we all agreed upon a criterion, it would imply that we are able to pick out a time in the pregnancy at which the "creature" begins to be human. which means that at a particular point in time it is a human being, but just a split second before [whatever is now considered to be human] was subhuman. However, since the development is gradual and slow ("continuous" if you will), the biological difference between the "already human" creature and the "still not human" is nil or negligible, which is absurd (calling one of two practically identical creatures "human," and the other, "subhuman").

We can now sum up the result of our discussion in this section by saying that the effort to search for a beginning to "human life" is futile (philosophically self destructing), and that the only way to view the formation of "human life" is as a *process*. Its "last chapter" is normally initiated by copulation between two humans of opposite sexes, continues via the uniting of the sperm and the egg, the sticking of the fertilized egg to the side of the womb and undergoing various metamorphoses, and culminates with birth. Now, if we are unable to establish where "human life" begins, how can we apply the SHL principle (now that we know that it cannot be automatically applied with respect to "potential human life")? And if we do not know when to apply the SHL principle, what kind of tools do we have to deal with the legal aspect of abortion? I will answer this question (in the next chapter), but not before saying a few more things in criticism of the pro-life philosophy. *(NO, MY DEAR DEAR PRO-LIFERS, I AM NOT THROUGH WITH YOU YET!)*

The Religious Philosophy Underlying The Pro-lifers Dogma.

The only religious rationale I can find behind the dogma "human life begins at conception" is that the [accident of the] joining together of the sperm and the egg is an indication of the will of God to create a human being. And if God gives life, who are we to take it away? The assumption underlying this rationale is that whatever happens reflects the will of God. In fact, not too many generations ago people went to fight sword duels to determine justice (trial by combat). If the combat resulted in the killing of person B by person A, that was an indication that A was right and B was wrong. That is to say, before the duel we could not tell who was right and who was wrong, but God, through the outcome of the duel, has shown us the light, and now we know [who was right (the victor!) and who was wrong (the victim!)]. I am not sure how many people today would think that way, but I would guess not too many.

But let us consider an actual example. Suppose there is a road accident where a person is seriously injured. He is brought to the hospital. Should the doctors attempt to save his life? Well, applying the above religious principle, the fact that he had the accident should reveal to us that God wanted him to die, so "who are we (the doctors) to intervene in God's doings and try to reverse His will (regarding the injured)?" To answer that, it could be argued that God had his reasons to cause the injury, maybe to punish this person, to warn him, or simply to make life more dramatic (who knows?) but in fact He did not intend to kill this person, and He saves him via the doctors' action. (It is understood that without the medical treatment the person would die.) God actually gave humans the knowledge of medicine so that they could save lives that would otherwise be lost. Doctors are nothing but middlemen who affect the final will of God (saving the person's life), whether this (final) will existed right from the start (the occurrence of the accident and the resulting injury) or whether God had been "thinking it over," and on second thought changed His mind as to the injured's fate (saving his life instead of destroying it). Now, if we accept the explanation regarding the road accident, why shouldn't we use the very same explanation regarding conception and abortion. God gave humans the knowledge to perform abortions (and why did He do this if He did not want us to use this knowledge?) When an accident happens in the form of unwanted pregnancy, we could reverse the results of the accident (exactly what the doctors are doing regarding the injured person in the road accident) and terminate the pregnancy. It works as if *GOD GIVES LIFE THROUGH THE PENIS OF THE IMPREGNATOR AND TAKES IT AWAY THROUGH THE HANDS (AND SKILL) OF THE ABORTIONIST.*

From the above it follows that, by its general philosophy, religion does not really have any argument or rationale to oppose abortion. In fact, the Jewish religion, albeit not condoning abortion, does not consider it the equivalent of murder, simply because the fetus is not regarded as a person.[6] All in all there is no general principle in religious philosophy that would imply that "human life begins at conception." It is a dogma that stands by itself.

---

[6] Apropos of the Jewish religion and birth control, it seems that the Jewish religious laws are designed to encourage procreation. This could be explained by the need for the survival of a nation in a diaspora under the constant threat of extermination. Since religious duty in general falls on men it is the Jewish men who are forbidden to "waste sperm" and therefore cannot use *coitus interruptus* (or masturbate, for that matter; even night ejaculation has to be dealt with in a specific manner). Females are not subject to most religious laws, and there is no prohibition against their use of birth control devices. As stated before, abortion is not condoned but is not regarded as murder.

The Case Where "Pro-life" Kills.

Now I intend to show how adoption of the dogma "human life begins at conception" actually acts as a human-life destroyer rather than as a human-life preserver. Consider the case of *in-vitro* fertilization. Medicine is now advanced enough (by God's will or against it?) to offer a technique designed to make happy parents out of couples, who without this technique would be childless. It works like this. The man's sperm and the woman's eggs are brought together in a test tube, where provisions are made to enhance the chance of fertilization. Under these ideal conditions it often happens that several eggs become fertilized. In order for the pregnancy to succeed it is necessary to select one egg that has the best chance of survival and implant it in the woman's womb, where it continues to develop exactly as during a normal pregnancy. All the eggs that are not selected are disposed of. Now, even though the fertilization was done artificially, and those unused fertilized eggs are out of the womb to start with, the fact that they are disposed of is so unacceptable to the pro-lifers that they oppose the entire procedure. Now, the procedure produces a baby, and without the procedure there would be no baby. The pro-lifers opt for "no-baby," — namely, no healthy baby for caring parents who would otherwise be childless — this only to protect their dogma. In pragmatic terms, using the pro-lifers' own language, *they choose to kill the baby in order to save the dogma.* In the eyes of the pro-lifers, the dogma even prohibits letting useless,

artificially formed fertilized eggs die naturally ***in vitro,*** where they were formed to start with. This is the true face of the "pro-life" movement which, as I have mentioned before, makes it more deserving of the title "pro-dogma" (making each pro-lifer a pro-dogmaer). While transferring the "sanctity of life" principle from the land of the living to the land of the potentials, the pro-lifers would not do the same with regards to the principle of self-defense. If they did, they would allow this potential baby to claim self-defense against the other fertilized eggs, which endanger its survival.

An In-depth Summary Note

It would be helpful to conclude this chapter by going more in depth into the difference between my philosophy and the pro-lifers'. A persuasive secular way to present the pro-life position (coinciding with the "little psychological pro-lifer" in the conscience of each and every one of us) would be to start with the end product, the (obviously-human) born baby and work backwards in time in small intervals (in "slow motion"—so to speak), claiming that due to continuity the humanness of the unborn in a given stage implied its humanness in the previous stage. This works all the way to conception, thus implying personhood at conception. This approach erroneously regards all the "frames" as ***one and the same entity in different points in time,*** that is, it regards, say, a half-month-old-worm-like embryo as "the baby 8½ months before birth," on account of the biological continuity (even though all the baby and embryo have in common is the genetic codification).[7] Abortion then becomes murder since it destroys a "–8½ (minus eight and a half)-month-old baby." My (pragmatic-social rather then biological) philosophy contends that, setting aside religious mystique, the significant thing about the embryo is not what it is, but rather what it would become (namely that it would become a baby).[8] Hence *the damage caused by abortion is not what it does to the embryo, but rather what it does to the baby* (preventing its birth). But the very same damage (preventing a birth of an otherwise born baby) is caused by contraception and abstention. Consequently, if we do not discriminate by codification (to condone murder at random) we are lead to the ultimate pro-lifer's position imposing upon us the duty to "screw to the last breath" (see box on page 37). If the pro-lifers find it impossible to live by such rules, then they must understand the refusal of unwillingly pregnant women to live by their rules.

---

[7] We know that the A-bomb consists of two substances that once "mixed" create a chain reaction. We can continuously decrease their quantities to get smaller and smaller bombs, but if we come below the minimum required for the chain reaction, the "new creature" is no longer a bomb (since it can't explode), but rather "building materials for a bomb." Likewise the embryo only constitutes "building materials for a person" rather than "a person." To use the continuity correctly one must not look at the personhood of the unborn as a dichotomy (yes or no), but rather assign a measure to it, equal to one (or 100%) at birth and decreasing continuously up to zero at conception. Decreasing it linearly would make the half-month-old embryo a 5.5% (or 1/18) person (that is, 94.5% non-person).

[8] For more details see pages 105 and 106.

Chapter III

The Legal Aspect of Abortion

Tools For A Solution

Equipped with the philosophical-moral back-ground as presented so far, we are now able to attempt to determine the legal standing of abortion in a [secular] progressive society. To phrase it differently, but equivalently, we want to decide what kind of protection should be given to the unborn — namely, to a creature starting as a fertilized egg at conception, and maturing to a full fledged baby at birth — at each stage of its development. Since we already established that any criterion adopted to determine when "full-fledged humanity" starts would be subjective, artificial, arbitrary and philosophically self-contradictory, this task, at least on the face of it, seems to be extremely difficult, if not impossible. It would make sense to start from a consensus, namely:

(1) A split second before fertilization, neither the egg nor the sperm deserves to be protected (this even the pro-lifers don't deny).

(2) A split second after birth the creature, now a baby, deserves full protection (this, even the pro-choicers don't deny).

Now, the process whereupon sperm and egg combine to become fertilized egg (a potential human of a more advanced degree), embryo, fetus, and finally a baby, is a gradual process (or to use more mathematical language pragmatically "continuous"), where nothing happens instantaneously, except maybe at both ends (fertilization and birth), when the graduality (continuity) sort of breaks down, in my opinion, not really breaks down but only roughens. At the birth end, if a freshly born baby is "human," it would make little sense to say that minutes before birth it was not, and therefore not deserving of protection. Biologically speaking, except for the trauma of the change of environment (from inside to outside the womb), no radical biological changes occur that should affect the creature's "humanness." At the fertilization end, there is indeed *prima facie* an apparent drastic change. Yet, in terms of the biological "potential human" substance, we can view conception as an exchange of a half billion or so sperm and one unfertilized egg, with one constantly multiplying fertilized egg. Thus we do not really have an instantaneous increase in the quantity of the "potential human" substance.

To strengthen our argument about the (albeit rough) gradual change at the conception end, we must go back to the Star Wars Contraceptive (SWC). When we presented the SWC we saw that, pragmatically speaking, it is equivalent to abortion, but dogmatically (according to the pro-lifers), those who used it would not be committing the crime of destroying a "human being," which supposedly occurs with abortion. Now, suppose that the SWC instead of acting immediately preceding fertilization, would act *upon* it: namely, the sperm is already inside the egg, but the SWC "holds its throat" and prevents the egg from developing. Biologically speaking, does this little technical variation make such a difference that it should radically change the issue? Intellectual honesty compels us to say *NO.* Suppose now that the arrest of the egg's development occurs after it becomes four cells strong, or eight cells strong, or ... 256 cells strong, or what should be the cut-off point? Well, each time there is just a minor gradual change, and at no stage would it be objectively correct to set a cut-off point. Now, there are already in the market contraceptives acting in a similar way, namely, preventing the (already fertilized) egg from developing normally. Other contraceptives, like the IUD, are doing a similar job, probably preventing the fertilized egg from sticking to the side of the womb. From a public opinion poll I took on an individual basis, I found that many people who do not favor abortion, would still go along with the IUD or a similarly working contraceptive. I guess a secular way to view the conception is not to look at it in MICRO, that is, as an instantaneous act of "sperm meets egg," but rather in MACRO, that is, to view the chain of events starting from intercourse and lasting for x number of days until pregnancy is detected as *one occurrence.* (Remember also that the sperm may wander about the vagina several days before fertilizing the egg.) If, at the end of this "occurrence" the woman is not pregnant (namely, conception did not take place) then we really "do not care to know" the reason. It may be because the sperm did not manage to reach the egg, either by nature or because of contraception; or the sperm may have reached the egg and fertilized it, but the development of the fertilized egg was arrested, by nature or by contraception; or perhaps the egg did not stick to the side of the womb, again due to nature or because of contraception. In fact this occurrence is only observable as one unit, where to start with the woman knows she is not pregnant, and after x number of days she knows she is. From her angle, the impregnation (the transition between a state of "no conception" to the state of "conception") was not the instantaneous meeting of the sperm and the egg, but rather a process lasting x number of days, starting from her knowing she was not pregnant and ending at her knowing that she was. By this approach *the beginning of the pregnancy is also a process.* Thus, we have established graduality also on the initiating end of the process of the formation of human life.

In order to proceed to the practical application of our just-established conclusion that the *whole* process of formation of human life is gradual (including its beginning and its end) we need to introduce a principle.

P/G	***PRINCIPLE OF GRADUALITY ("CONTINUITY"):*** SOCIETY IN ITS LEGISLATION (AND MORAL JUDGMENT) SHOULD — TO THE EXTENT FEASIBLE — TREAT GRADUALLY DEVELOPING THINGS IN A GRADUAL MANNER.

This principle is used in quite a number of occasions in our society. For instance in the determination of income taxes, where the more income you have, the more taxes you pay. Another example is that of fines for exceeding speed limits (as is customary in several states) where for each mile above the speed limit you pay, say five dollars. Applying the Principle of Graduality (P/G) to the protection of the life of the "potential human" during the course of the pregnancy, we can deduce that since the unfertilized egg has no protection, then because of graduality also the fertilized egg should have no protection. By the same token, since the born baby has full (100%) protection, so should the "potential human," slightly before birth. The measure of protection has therefore to increase in some way from zero at (and slightly after) conception to 100% at (and slightly before) birth. The problem now is how many "stages" of protection we can feasibly find, and at what points of the pregnancy they should be set. We will come back to deal with this problem after we inquire into all the factors society has to take into consideration when deciding about its policy regarding abortion.

Deciding Factors In The Politics of Abortion.

Society is more than a mere collection of individuals. It is a self-managing body, a business if you like. It has legitimate "selfish" (in the collective sense) interests and is expected to take care of these interests in a rational manner. Its duty to protect is, in fact, not limited to the protection of some individuals from others, but rather goes beyond that to the protection of society at large as a collective body, and protection not only from outside factors, but also from the actions of its own members. One of those interests is the demographic interest, which, under certain conditions, may compel the society to intervene in demographic processes and take actions to control the number of its members. It may work in two different directions. A society whose death rate exceeds the birth rate to an alarming degree, may be driven to take drastic measures in order to close the gap, or else face the threat of becoming extinct or too weak to survive. Such a society may restrict or prohibit abortion, and for that matter other contraceptives, not on moral grounds, but rather on pragmatic grounds. Conceivably, in the extreme case, this society may even force fertile women into pregnancy. Where, on the other hand, a society is too big, and an increase in numbers would drive it into a population explosion (or in the less extreme case would drastically reduce an already low standard of living), then this society would be compelled to encourage birth control devices, abortion included. It may even opt for forced abortions or even killing babies upon birth. China, which is such a society, practices a policy whereby couples with more than one child are punished severely, women are coerced if not forced to abort, and occasionally newborns are killed.

Society may also lend itself to "moral" considerations to reflect the attitude of its members where it comes to protection of unborns. Clearly, society is only obligated to protect its full-fledged human members. If and when it chooses to protect lesser creatures, it is expanding its activity beyond its required duty. Here, emotions to humans are extended to creatures lesser than humans, where they too are given some protection. This protection, however, is limited, and constitutes a lesser protection than the protection accorded to humans. For example, we protect animals from torture but are permitted to use them for medical experimentation even if torture is involved. The very lives of animals are not protected, and owners can "put their pets to sleep" at will. The protection of unborns, which are only potential humans, should be viewed similarly. Whatever protection they are given, however, comes only as a result of good-will gesture, and must be considered secondary to the primary duty society has to its full-fledged human members, including women. It is only towards the end of the pregnancy, when the human potentiality of the unborn is high enough (**but not before that**) that its "right to life" competes with the right of women to autonomy and quality of life (presumably a lesser right than the right to life) to the extent that it presents society with a dilemma.

Now, this discrimination between humans and potential humans as well as between potential humans at various stages is not the only discrimination practiced in society. We discriminate even between existing members of society by age. If you are a minor you cannot vote, and if you are under 16, you may not drive a car nor may you have sex with an adult without exposing this adult to the risk of being charged with statutory rape. In most states you have to be 21 to buy liquor.

As we already established that the right to life for humans does not automatically extend to potential humans, then what should the moral (and consequently legal) status of potential humans be? Well, the moral aspect should be viewed as follows: In order to win the "right to life," namely, to become an actual human, the potential human has to undergo a chain of occurrences, namely, overcome a chain of obstacles. First, when it starts as a half-gener (sperm), it must, against all odds (namely with infinitely small probability), combine with another half-gener in the form of an egg. Then, the resulting potential human, the fertilized egg, must succeed in sticking to the side of the womb, divide and so on. At no stage is there a guarantee of success; all there is, is a probability the egg will develope into a baby. In our present technologically developed society, the potential human has to overcome many more obstacles in the form of the various contraceptives. In practice, this means that the probabilities of sperm surviving the contraceptive and still reaching the egg, or of the egg sticking to the side of the womb, are drastically decreased. Now, what the pro-choicers are saying is that, in addition to all those obstacles, the potential human must overcome one more. *It has to obtain the consent of the would-be mother to have him, or else be aborted.* That is to say, *it cannot emigrate from the realm of potentials into the realm of the actuals without a transit visa in the form of the approval of its "carrier," the would-be mother* (as well as the approval of society, in the case of a society with a strong demographic interest in limiting the size of the population), the same way not every human on the face of the earth (even though all people are equal in the eyes of the Lord) can freely emigrate from his Third World land to the United States of America. Not that the U.S. cannot afford to absorb, say, 250 million miserable people, who could improve their subhuman standard of living and live decently by emigrating from their poor country to the U.S., but the U.S. does not feel obligated to do so because this would hurt the standard of living of the now existing

Americans. Thus, from its own selfish material considerations about maintaining its standard of living, the U.S. does not allow unrestricted immigration. By the same token, existing, or actual, people should be entitled to restrict immigration to their realm, from the realm of the potential people, when accepting these "immigrants" would impose on their quality of life. That applies both to the pregnant woman as well as to society at large. A Mexican does not become a (legal) American citizen just by managing to cross a river or climb over barbed wire. Likewise, a potential human does not earn the right to become actual just because it manages to circumvent contraceptives and (winning the lottery) becomes a full-gener (fertilized egg) out of two half-geners (the sperm and the unfertilized egg).

In our medically developed world children should not be the results of accidents (or lotteries), but rather the fruits of the free will of loving parents. It is in our power, and it is our right as a society, to reverse the result of the accident, and only allow those potential humans that we really want to immigrate to our real world. This is true both for the would-be parents as well as for the society at large, because it is statistically well known that unwanted children have a greater chance of becoming undesirable members of society, poor and requiring public assistance, at best, or criminals, at worst. Society has just so much duty — if any at all — to go out of its way to act against its own interest on behalf of the "morality" of preserving potential human life. And its duty is even less, if any, when protecting potential life would conflict with its other undisputed duties such as the duty to preserve the liberty of its full-fledged female members and protect them from rape; and rape here means not only a forcible use of the woman's body (in particular her vagina) by an individual to satisfy his sexual desires, but also a forcible use of the woman's body (in particular her womb) by society (requiring her to carry a baby) to satisfy the ["ethical" or religious] desires of some fanatic individuals, who happen to have influence with the legislator. The truth is, that if society had the obligation of preserving any potential human, it could not survive. This would not only mean forcing everybody to have sex all the time, but also cloning all existing members, once this technique becomes available[1], since every cell of each of us constitutes a unique genetic code (configuration), which would be lost forever upon our death. This cell is obviously a human being by the definition of the pro-lifers.

The right of women (or society when applicable) to control or regulate procreation has another very important aspect. The main characteristic that makes human beings superior to other creatures is our intelligence. Among other things, our intelligence gives us the ability to manipulate nature thus allowing us to achieve better control over our lives than animals have. We have made ourselves, to a great extent,

---

[1] Furthermore, to be fully devoted to the cause, society should halt any project it is now involved in so it can concentrate all its intellectual and financial means to discover the technique for cloning.

"weather proof" by having homes equipped with heating and cooling devises to keep us warm in the cold winter and cool in the hot summer. We can stock up refrigerators so that we do not have to go hunting every day or else starve to death. Medicine can, in many cases, fix our bodies when their normal operation is frustrated either by nature or by accidents. Not only can we cure many diseases or transplant organs, but we can also forge pregnancies that are impossible by nature, to accommodate women who desire to become mothers, and by contrast, terminate unwanted pregnancies. Thus, unlike animals, which once they conceive must carry and give birth, women do have a choice regarding their procreative function. To require them to give up that choice is to require them *to degrade their human existence* (characterized by having choices) *into animal existence* (characterized by having no choices). *How ironic, that those who wish to impose such degredation on women do so in the name of pro-human-life!*

The Solution At Last

It is convenient at this point to concisely summarize the conclusion we have reached thus far, so that we will be able to proceed to the completion of our task of determining the legal standing of abortion. The conclusions are these:

(1) We have liberated ourselves from the need to determine the "beginning of human life" by

accepting the fact that it is a *process* (going back all the way to the primates).

(2) We have recognized that every criterion for determining "humanness" (viability, distinguishability, or recognition of the face, formation of the main part of the brain, to name a possible few), would not only be subjective, arbitrary, and accepted by only part of society, while rejected by the other part, but also self-destructive because of the graduality or continuity of the process (now a human being, a second earlier not?).

(3) We established graduality or "continuity [not only during pregnancy but also] at both ends of the pregnancy and deduced from it that immediately following conception the potential baby does not deserve any protection, while immediately preceding birth it deserves full protection.

(4) We reiterated the duty of society to protect the quality of life of its members.

(5) We reiterated the right of any female member of society to protection and autonomy.

Faced with all these conclusions (some seem to contradict the others), what is society to do? Well, it can adopt either one of the three following approaches:

No mutual obligation: Here we say that even though members of society are prohibited from harming each other, no member of society is obligated to go out of his/her way, not even an inch, to save the life of another member. Thus, if somebody's life is in danger (e.g., if he or she is in a burning house, drowning in a river, or injured in an automobile accident), one is under no obligation to take any affirmative action in order to save this person's life, not even to call 911. In that case even if the unborn is considered a full-fledged person, the woman can abort at any stage of the pregnancy, since she is not obligated to take any action, such as continuing her pregnancy, in order to save the unborn's life.

Limited mutual obligation: Here we assume that society is not only a mutually protective body, that is, a collection of individuals under contractual obligation not to harm each other; but also a limited mutually insuring body, where each member, to a limited extent, undertakes the obligation to go somewhat out of his/her way in order to save another person's life, with the understanding that if that member's own life is in danger, society enforces the contract on others, putting them under the obligation to come to his/her rescue, even at the expense of their convenience (up to a certain point). Thus, you have the obligation to call 911 when another person's life is on the line, and you may even be forced by law to transport an injured person to the hospital in your car, and may be even to donate blood. But you are not obligated to donate your kidney, or stay for nine months in the hospital infusion-connected to this person. In this case, even if the unborn is to be considered a full-fledged person, a pregnant woman would not be obligated to stay pregnant unwillingly; that is, she has the right to abortion, except when we come close enough to birth where the inconvenience to her is marginal.

Total (or substantial) mutual obligation: Here each person is required to totally (or substantially) surrender his or her convenience to save lives of others, including being infusion-connected to them for nine months, or taking them out of burning houses or rivers at the risk of one's life. In that case if the unborn is to be considered a full-fledged person, then abortion could be prohibited. This is, however, inconsistent with the now-existing legal statute where people *are not required* to contribute their body parts, not even to donate blood for the benefit of other people's lives.

But even if it were so, that is, the state did have such power over the autonomy of its citizens, there is still the question of whether the unborn is indeed to be considered a full-fledged person. Since this is very much in dispute, and since in cases where absolute justice is undefinable the only justice is the pragmatic justice, namely, the justice of compromise, then it follows that society should forge a compromise or a balance between all the conflicting interests in the debate.

There are three sets of interests to be balanced:

(1) The right of the would-be mother to liberty (autonomy) versus the right of the would-be baby to life;

(2) The attitudes or principles of the pro-lifers versus the attitude or principles of the pro-choicers; and

(3) The quality of life of the society versus its "extended moral compulsion."

Luckily enough, the interests of the unwillingly pregnant woman, the pro-choicers attitude, and the quality-of-life requirement of society, all merge together to be on one side of the balance; whereas the interests of the unborn, the pro-life attitude, and the "moral" consideration of society, merge together to lie on the other. Thus we have to balance only two contrasting interests. Now, since at the beginning of the pregnancy we must, as deduced, permit abortion, whereas at the end of the pregnancy we must prohibit it, then there must be a point of time in the course of the pregnancy where permission ends and prohibition starts, which we will name here the **critical point,** or the **cut-off point.** Since every criterion was declared to be subjective and arbitrary, then how do we go about setting it? Well, here I can offer my services as a mathematician-statistician to determine the most objective balance. The objectivity is translated into mathematics as the assignment of equal weight to the contrasting interests. This determines the compromised critical (cut-off) point to be exactly midway between conception and birth, namely at 4½ months into the pregnancy.[2] Therefore, we should permit abortion in the first half of the pregnancy and prohibit it thereafter (in the second half).[3] However, due to the principle of graduality (continuity), we may smooth out the transition between permission and prohibition by spreading it along the second half of the second trimester, where abortion could have some restrictions put on them, starting from mandatory consultation, with the woman having the final word, and ending with her having to obtain permission from a judge or a non-religious committee (except that under special compelling circumstances she would still be entitled to abortion by law). The state may prohibit abortion at the third trimester. To conclude, the statistical solution combined with the Principle of Graduality calls for abortion on demand during the first half of the pregnancy, authority of the state to prohibit abortion during the last trimester, and a

---

[2] The same solution can also be obtained graphically. See Graph 1 next page.

[3] I must reiterate that the solution I offer here is not one I personally favor. It completely ignores the principle of choice discussed in chapter I, as well as the superiority of the woman to the unborn on account of her being an existing person, which should entitle her to a greater weight (e.g., giving her double weight would shift the cut-off point from the middle of the second trimester to its end). It only represents what results when one applies the principle of graduality with equal weight. Furthermore, to be perfectly honest, the assignment of equal weight is mathematically just as arbitrary as any other assignment of weight. Psychologically, however, it seems that fifty-fifty is the fairest assignment since it gives equality with "no prior conditions." Note also that this solution does not even have to assume the constitutional right of women to control their bodies.

GRAPH 1
(THE GRAPHIC REPRESENTATION OF THE SOLUTION)

A better understanding of the statistically compromised balancing of the right of the mother versus the right of the unborn, could be reached by a graphical representation of the one against the other. Here it is assumed that the right of the unborn increases linearly from its 0% point at conception to its 100% point at its birth, while the right of the mother decreases linearly from its 100% at conception to 0% at birth. As long as the line representing the right of the mother is above the one representing the right of the unborn (that is, the measure of her right is greater than the one for the unborn), then her right takes precedence; otherwise this of the unborn does. After three months of pregnancy (x=3) the unborn's right (point A) reads 33.3% and that of the mother (point B) reads 66.7%; that is, the mother's right take precedence. After six months the right of the mother (point C) reads 33.3%, while that of the unborn (point D) reads 66.7%, and thus the unborn's right take precedence. At four and a half months (point E) both rights equal 50%, which means that before that point the mother's right takes precedence and after it, the unborn's right does. This is our statistical solution to the problem.

RIGHT OF MOTHER AND UNBORN

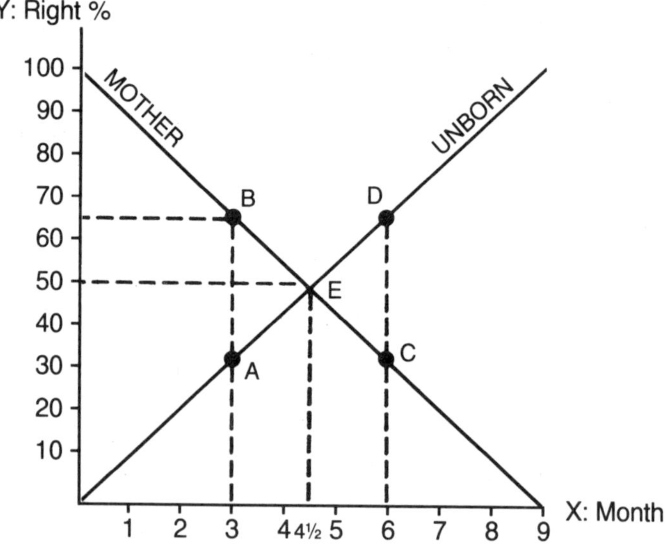

transition period with restrictions gradually increasing in between. This compromise, albeit not giving the woman full control of her body at all times during pregnancy, which the pro-choicers demand, is still fair to the woman to the extent that it gives her enough of an opportunity to have an abortion at the time when it is medically most feasible. If she does not take advantage of it within the first half of the pregnancy she really wouldn't be as morally justified to cry RAPE (by society) as she would if the pregnancy was forced upon her from the start. It would be reasonable for society to tell a woman in the last trimester of her pregnancy: "Listen baby! If by your own choice you carried the fetus that long, then you should walk just one extra mile, and give it a chance to life. It is really a shame to 'waste' a baby so close to being born, not only for its sake but also for the sake of all of those who seek to adopt a child."

Now, this is not what the pro-choicers want, because it violates their principle of the woman having full control of her body at all times, but it is a compromise most can live with. What they get in return is blocking the pro-lifers' ability to force their unreasonable and impractical dogma that "human life begins at conception." The pro-lifers should realize that they are not messengers of God (He has ways to impose His will) and cannot legally force upon the society at large moral principles on which there is not only no consensus, but which are actually accepted by much less than half of the population. They can try to influence others by spreading their message, but no more. They should be content with the fact that they would not really have lost the war, since fetuses that are close enough to constitute human life would be saved. For society, the solution offered is also optimal. There would be no need to change a situation already existing as a *fait accompli* due to the 1973 *Roe vs. Wade* Supreme Court ruling. (Since the vast majority of abortions are performed in the first trimester of the pregnancy, *Roe vs. Wade* settled the entire problem of abortion with the exception of only a few cases.) The compromise would protect women also from the need to resort to dangerous and expensive illegal abortions, which they would surely resort to if abortions became illegal altogether. In addition it is a very plausible solution to the emotional issue of abortion, not simply because it fairly and, as objectively as possible, balances the interests of the unwillingly pregnant woman and her unborn, but also because it roughly coincides in actuality with some other major logical criteria (such as the development of the brain, which occurs in the beginning of the third trimester) as well as with *Roe vs. Wade.*

So far as *Roe vs. Wade* is concerned, even though it is an optimal fair solution pragmatically and ideologically (the idea of balancing conflicting interests), the particular criterion it is based upon, *viability,* on top of being arbitrary and subjective, is also, in a way, self-contradictory. It is as if society is telling the pregnant woman: "Since the fetus is now viable, that is, it can breath by itself, or in general survive independent of you, then you need to carry it." To this any intelligent woman could respond: "Well, if it can survive by itself, then if you, society, want it, you are welcome to have it. Take it out of my body (either by induced labor or by Cesarian section, to name two methods used to accomplish this) and let it survive by itself in an incubator. I do not want any part of it, and I absolutely refuse to serve as a living substitute for a hospital incubator for a potential baby I do not want and you, society, insist on having. Now, if this cannot be done: that is, if you cannot make the thing survive on its own without me, then it is not really viable. Since it is not viable then the criterion you applied to make me carry the fetus is not satisfied. Since the criterion is not satisfied, then I am entitled to an abortion."

Despite the use of subjective and self-contradictory criterion, the pragmatic result, of *Roe vs. Wade* roughly coincides with my theoretical result, which is the most objective possible, being based on a statistical balance that disregards the merits of the case. *Roe vs. Wade* however goes beyond just balancing interests and setting the cut-off point. It establishes the right of a woman to control her body, regarding the specific aspect of pregnancy, as a *basic constitutional right* — absolute and unconditional during the first trimester of the pregnancy, and subject to some restrictions during the second. This for a long time has taken care of all the political hustle and bustle and hypocrisy surrounding the issue. The recent Supreme Court rulings (which weaken and all but reverse *Roe vs. Wade*) are extremely regrettable, causing the nation to waste its energy on issues irrelevant to daily life instead of solving its urgent problems (and there is no lack of them!). It is my wish that the Supreme Court would reverse this course for the benefit of this great country of ours.

Both *Roe vs. Wade* and my statistical solution give the first trimester to the woman, and the third to the unborn. But whereas *Roe vs. Wade* permits the state to impose restrictions after 90 days, the statistical solution defers them for another 45 days. We can use the statistical solution in combination with the democratic process and ask the public, by referendum, to pick a number greater than 137 (4½ months) as its favorable cut-off point between permission and restriction or prohibition. (The numbers represent day counts from the beginning of the pregnancy.) The average, or median, of those numbers would be the "choice of the community" for the critical (cut-off) point. It is important to note first that the issue should be brought *directly to the people,* so that it can be separated from politics, thus releasing politicians from addressing this disturbing issue. Secondly, it is important to remember that even for practical reasons alone the public should have no access to the woman's domain during the first trimester. This is really the minimal period of time the woman needs in order first to discover that she is pregnant, then to make up her mind as to whether or not she wishes to terminate the pregnancy, and finally, if she decides to terminate, to make the proper convenient arrangement for the procedure of abortion to take place. This, as already said, is a *basic constitutional issue,* and should not be decided on a local or simply popular basis. It makes no sense that between two American women, one living in Atlanta, say, the other one in New York City, there would be an essential (more than marginal) difference as to their rights to their bodies.

Abortion — a Contraceptive Substitute?

To end this chapter I must answer criticisms of "abortion on demand" on the grounds that it is being "abused" as a substitute for contraceptive use. The contention of such critics is that "using abortion as a contraceptive device is morally wrong," and that "any woman wishing not to get pregnant should either abstain or else use contraceptives," and that "those who do not (or who use contraceptives unsuccessfully) should suffer the consequences and carry the unborn to term." This contention has no merit, *none whatsoever.* The only logical reasoning to object to the use of abortion as a birth control method would be to show that it is harmful in some way. We therefore have to examine it from the point of view of all the parties involved. There are two such parties, the woman and the unborn. From the woman's point of view, it is really her own business as to which kind of birth control method to use — abstention, the pill, IUD, or abortion — as much so as her diet is. From the unborn's point of view there may be two considerations, one minor, one major. The minor one is the possible pain involved in the process. Now at the very early stages of fetal development, where the brain and the nerve system are not developed enough to transfer and receive (feel) pain, this question is irrelevant. If a fertilized egg can feel pain, maybe also the unfertilized egg or sperm can, in which case, every contraceptive causes pain. Otherwise, the duration of the pain (before the object dies) is quite short and in substance is equivalent to the pain caused by injection, which is obviously (because of the duration) less than the pain caused by circumcision. At any rate it is outweighed by far by the pain that the unwanted pregnancy causes to the woman. The major consideration of the unborn is its right to life. But this right to life is no more violated if it is taken away by abortion than if it is taken away by contraception. This potential human is only interested in one thing: "Am I going to live or die?" It makes no difference to it if it is prevented from coming into this world by the diaphragm, the condom, or through abortion, it only makes a difference to the pro-lifers because of their dogma.

Ironically enough, if it does make a difference, then how come the pro-lifers are exactly the ones who are the most fanatic opponents of sex education and thus are the main culprits for unwanted teen-age pregnancies, one of the major contributors to the statistics of abortions? What hypocrisy!

Moreover, if we consider with intellectual honesty the question of preventing potential humans from materializing into actual humans, "baby killing" in the pro-lifers' terminology, then we must admit that a nun, say, is more of a "baby killer" than a mother of three who is having an abortion in order not to become a mother of four (because she can't afford it economically, physically, or psychologically). This mother has already given life to three human beings, *the nun — to none!* That is, the nun, by her abstention, prevented the birth of several human beings she could otherwise have given life to. What difference does it make whether this prevention was done by contraceptives, abortion, or abstention?

We can recruit fantasy to help us illustrate this idea as follows:

"In the land of the unmaterialized souls, side by side with the souls of the aborted children, each of whom points a finger to his would-be mother saying: 'Mother! You killed me!' there are the unmaterialized souls of the never-conceived children of the nuns, who also point their fingers to their would-be mothers, the nuns, saying the exact same thing ('Mother! You killed me!')"

My mother, who is not in favor of abortion, told me once while discussing that issue that while she was pregnant with my younger sister (T, by her first initial), she was considering abortion because of the economic situation of the family. "Now" — says she — "suppose I did go through the abortion, then you wouldn't have your sister T". "True" — I answered

— "but suppose you never used any birth control devices, I would most likely have a few more sisters like T. Why is their prevention from materializing through the use of contraceptives less of a waste than the would-be prevention of the materialization of my sister T via abortion?"

Summary

To forge a legal stand on the abortion issue one must first consider the ***principal of choice,*** under which a person legally belongs to oneself and, unless by consent, his or her body cannot be used by society (e.g., requiring this person to donate biological substance, take risks, or considerably compromise one's quality of life) to save or maintain the life of another. Applied to women, this principle entitled them to abortion even if the unborn is a person, the end of pregnancy being the only possible exception. Those, who despite all the many legal precedents choose to ignore this principle, are reminded that, in addition the personhood of the unborn is very much in dispute, and that even under these unjustifiable (inconsistent with the existing legal status) harsh circumstances a compromise is called for. The most objective statistical compromise ensures abortion on demand during the first half of the pregnancy, and allows prohibition in the third trimester. This exception (prohibition) is, however, practically merely academic, as very few abortions are performed in the last trimester, most of those due to unusual compelling circumstances, and in many such cases the fetus can be saved.

Address to the Supreme Court:

Why Should *Roe vs. Wade* not be Reversed?[1]

The detrimental effect that a reversal of *Roe vs. Wade* would have on American politics was already mentioned in the introduction. It would divert the energy of politicians and the content of political campaigns from relevant and urgent issues to the single issue of abortion, which pragmatically, and by its nature (happening in the wombs of women away from society), is not a public issue. It becomes one only due to the aggressive activity of religious fundamentalists who sure know how to make waves. The detrimental effect on American women of such a reversal is also clear. It would send them back to back alleys and butchers' knives. However, inasmuch as the Supreme Court should take into consideration the pragmatic effect of its decisions on the nation, the effects of this decision may not be the deciding

---

[1] This was sent to all justices of the Supreme Court in August 1991.

factor if the consideration is in clear conflict with important principles. If on the other hand, a conflict does not exist or is not genuine, then the pragmatic consideration should prevail.

Now, the only reason the Supreme Court would have to throw the issue back to the political arena is judicial restraint. This means that in spite of the fact that seven out of nine justices in 1973 thought that there was a constitutional issue involved here, the present court may discard this possibility. Once it does that, abortion is no longer a constitutional issue. Under this condition, the court is prohibited by the Constitution to "take sides" because that makes it an unauthorized legislator.

Now, no matter whether you believe women have the right to their bodies or you don't, there can be no argument that this right (which is now in dispute) is *fundamental.* To see that this is so consider the cases of two women who desperately need an abortion. One lives in a democratic country (D) that prohibits abortion, the other in a totalitarian country (T) that permits it. It seems quite obvious that the fact that she can cast a vote every four years is not as relevant to the woman in country D, as the fact that she can't have the abortion she desperately needs. Her freedom to vote is dwarfed by her not being free to control her own body, a freedom fully enjoyed by her counterpart in country T. Freedom is worthless if it is only a slogan. It can only be measured by tangible application, especially when the need to exercise a freedom is current and urgent. Thus, if abortion is outlawed in any state of the union, women living in such states would be less free than their counterparts in a totalitarian country. This shows clearly that the right to abortion is indeed fundamental and as such should not be left to the states. It is unthinkable that two American women separated only by a state line could be so unequal in terms of such fundamental rights, which are given to one and denied the other. In addition, it is easier on the state level for well-organized minorities through pressure and unethical deals with politicians to pass laws not necessarily favored by the majority but nevertheless which bear the official stamp of representing "the majority of the electorate of the state of . . . ," thus having a clean bill of health before the Supreme Court for the purpose of judicial restraint.

Now, if the Supreme Court, without being compelled to by the Constitution, makes decisions that are genuinely contrary to the will of the people, indeed it commits the sin of becoming a legislator unconstitutionally. If, however, it would only appear that the court is "misbehaving," where, in fact, its decisions represent the will of the people and, furthermore, protect the will of the people from manipulating politicians, then the court is not committing the sin of overstepping its authority since democracy is not being defeated but rather served by its actions. This is exactly the case regarding the issue of abortion. The majority of Americans (remember the issue should be resolved on the national level) are pro-choice, and this fact is undisputed.[2] So that even if the court holds that there is no explicit constitutional right to choice, choice is still what most Americans want. For almost twenty years, one full generation, choice has been the law of the land. One may doubt the original justification for making choice the law of the land, but one must realize that it is now *deeply entrenched in our recent tradition and way of life.* So even if it is believed not to have been a fundamental right to begin with in 1973 (erroneously endowed then), *it is now.* As a general rule the Court should not be hasty to reverse itself, unless under compelling circumstances. Even less so in the particular case of *Roe vs. Wade,* which was rendered with an overwhelming majority of 7:2, and where the present compelling circumstances contribute all towards letting it stand rather than towards reversing it. A reversal here would mean taking away rights that are now taken for granted, constituting an integral part of our daily life. The Russians, who tasted only partial democracy for only a couple of years, resisted the gang of eight that tried to take their new freedoms away from them.

LET THE SUPREME COURT NOT BE THE GANG OF NINE TAKING AWAY CHOICE FROM AMERICAN WOMEN, WHO HAVE BEEN TASTING IT FOR A WHOLE GENERATION NOW. AND, IF THE COURT CAN FIND NO BETTER REASON, LET THE COURT LET THOSE WOMEN KEEP THIS RIGHT FOR THE SAKE OF THE STATUS QUO.

---

[2] They elected Bush as their president *not* because of his attitude about abortion, so that he is *not* their representative regarding this particular issue. This contradiction would not have taken place if the people were allowed to vote directly on issues that are self-contained, separated from all other issues and not requiring any professional knowledge; the President's opinion is only as good as anybody else's

---

Appendix

Response to Crum's Pro-Life Arguments[1]

PREFACE

The manuscript of my book was completed at the end of august 1991, but its publication was put off due to my travel overseas for several months. Upon my return, in April 1992, I was made aware of Crum's and McCormack's book. I enjoyed reading the book which intelligently and thoroughly covers the subject, and I have much respect for both authors. The pro-life position is presented by Crum in the first part of the book. His argument, for the most part meets academic standards, but at the same time is in many points flawed and misleading. This combination makes it an inspiration and a challenge for a good debate — an added dimension to my book. Even though most

---

[1] The arguments are presented in the first (pro-life) part of the two-part book: *Abortion, Pro-Choice or Pro-Life* by Gary Crum and Thelma McCormack, American University press 1992. The reader does not necessarily have to have this book in front of him or her in order to read this appendix since Crum's arguments are presented here as a part of the discussion.

83

of the responses to the arguments are already contained in my book, I have chosen not to incorporate the debate within the main text, but rather to leave my book intact and devote an entire appendix to the debate. Some of the ideas already brought up in my book will have to be reiterated, others expanded, and some new ideas will be introduced. I will discuss Crum's arguments in the same order that they appear in his book, sometimes at the cost of breaking up ideas to return to them at a later stage.

Crum's book is outstanding in that it attempts to be academic and secular (not withstanding that attempt, as will be shown, it does not quite accomplish the latter), and as such lends itself to discussion. I call it outstanding since most pro-lifers are religious and, as such, come to the arena armored with dogma (in this particular case, "life begin at conception") that is not negotiable. The only situation allowing argument with religious people on a principle, is when their belief is derived from a more comprehensive principle accepted by both sides, and you can prove to them that there is an error in the derivation. But "life begins at conception" is a principle of itself. The need for protection for the unborn, as claimed by the pro-lifers, is derived from the principle of "sanctity of human life." This derivation, however, is shown in my book to be deceptive, using a smoke screen. Crum at least attempts to "prove" the conception personhood scientifically. Yet, his over devotion to pure ethics, and his dogmatic approach in general, give his book a religious overtone and makes me wonder whether indeed his prejudices allow for the objectivity needed for scientific treatise. We also have to remember that the argument is about public policy, and the main difference between religion and pragmatic philosophy, is that the former is absolutely rigid, whereas the latest allows for flexibility, if not at the heart of the principle, at least at its margins. Crum's rigidity (which he probably would excuse as scientific consistency) even exceeds that of some religious pro-lifers. Let's now examine the book chapter by chapter.

Crum's Chapter I:
INTRODUCTION

Crum points out the confusion resulting from the difference in the names selected by the two parties to the debate, both for themselves as well as for their opponents. In order to be fair, he proposes calling each party by the name it prefers, "pro-life" for the pro-lifers and "pro-choice" for the pro-choicers. On the face of it, his proposal sounds fair but actually is not. By selecting its own name, each group means to say that its opponent is its negation: that is, by calling themselves pro-choice, the pro-choicers imply that their opponents are anti-choice, and by calling themselves pro-life, the pro-lifers imply that their opponents are anti-life. But whereas the pro-lifers admit that they are anti-choice (by saying that once pregnant, the woman should have no choice), the pro-choice deny being anti-life. They celebrate life, especially quality of life, both for women as well as for children (many of them are parents to children they love and care for). They are not even anti-life in terms of an unwanted fetus, but they refuse to accord it supremacy over quality of life, which includes the autonomy of the fetus' carriers, pregnant women. So, in fact, we do not achieve symmetry by Crum's supposedly fair selection of names. The damage caused as a result of this name selection, however, is propagandistic only, and thus tolerable.

Not so, when the name for the subject of the whole argument (the unborn) is selected. By calling the fetus an "unborn child" or an "unborn baby" Crum already assumes, and more than just psychologically, that it is a (full-fleged) human being, who has just a little problem with the cruel outside world because of the fact that it is yet unborn. This assumption, manifested throughout the book, defeats the purpose of the scientific objective analysis. I could live with the term "unborn" standing by itself, as this does not pre-characterize the subject but rather described an undisputed fact. What would suit our purpose is a biological term. Here, however, the richness of the English language (which supplies different names, embryo or fetus, according to the unborn's stage of development) becomes an obstacle. Therefore, the biological term "conceptus" should be used. Unlike the term "unborn baby", which is destined to play on our emotions, this is a neutral term describing a biological status. It does not imply or presuppose anything about the subject's personhood or the lack thereof, which is the very thing that is in dispute. Calling a child "a child" and an adult "an adult" does not imply that one of them is less or more of a human being than the other, only that we are talking of different stages of development. Thus calling the unborn "conceptus" does not say whether or not it is a human being, only that it is in a stage of development different from that of the child or the baby.

Inasmuch as this prejudicial name-calling is inconsistent with science, it is in line with the deceptive pro-life magic propaganda: They first only call it a baby, and before you know it treat it like one (i.e., they start with "it *is called* a baby," put up a smoke screen, and when the smoke screen is gone, the "called" is gone with it, and what's left is "it *is* a baby"). In other words, what they do boils down to: "let's call it a baby and win the debate." Crum is indeed more honest and sophisticated. He says: "Let's first regard it as a person, and only later, in chapter IV will we worry about showing that it really is (a person)." Yet, once he calls it a person, he believes all his problems are solved. He can, for example, talk about its human rights, which he believes should equal ours. He fails to see that if we endow any group in our society with human rights, we cannot do it at the expense of another group. For instance, when black people got voting rights, the right of whites to vote was not taken away. By contrast, the *only* way we can give rights to the conceptus is by depriving women of their rights. This is how the biological difference between a person, a biologically independent entity, and the fetus, a biologically dependent or parasitical entity, expresses itself pragmatically in terms of rights and thus prevents us from regarding the fetus (socially or legally) as a person. Therefore, the right (or lack thereof) of an entity to have rights is not acquired by semantics, that is, by what name we choose to call it, but rather by what it is. If Crum was faithful to his intention to be scientific, he would have (as he should) used the term "conceptus," and thus would have avoided much of the confusion and the distortion characterizing his treatise. As an example, at the bottom of page 50 Crum says: " All individual human beings, no matter what their age, sex, race and so forth, should by default be considered person until proven otherwise." We cannot apply this principle to the conceptus unless we arbitrarily decide that it is a human being, something we cannot prove to be a fact of life. But since Crum calls it a human being, then simply by semantics he "proves" to us, applying the above quoted principle, that it is a person.

Crum's Chapter II:
ETHICAL CONCEPTS AND
COMMON ABORTION ARGUMENTS

Crum introduces two schools of philosophers, teleological (or utilitarian), holding that "the end justifies the means," and deontological, holding that it does not, and thus stands, on a higher ethical plane.

In my opinion it makes little sense to use a criterion phrased in such a generality. After all, any normal person will sometimes act teleologically, and at other times act deontologically, depending on what is the end and what are the means[2]. To kill Hitler, in order to prevent the Holocaust, or to kill Sadam Hussein, in order to prevent the Gulf war (and thus prevent the death of hundreds of thousands), could be considered justifiable; whereas to kill a passer-by in order to rob him of $5 in order to donate to cancer research ought to be considered immoral. A pure deontologist would not even kill for self defense. I do not believe it is a principle one can survive with. But let us leave this dogmatic definition alone, with the understanding that the teleologists are essentially utilitarian or pragmatic, while the deontologists are "moralistic."

Crum now takes a few teleological pro-choice arguments and provides their pro-life responses.

Argument #1

Here it is claimed that abortions save tax money by decreasing the number of people on welfare or in jails. Crum admits the validity of the argument in the short run, but then he goes through a lengthy demographic analysis to show that in the long run, a generation away, these aborted would-be people would become tax payers (he forgets the high percentage of prisoners, unemployed, and welfare

---

[2] To go even deeper it is sometimes a matter of opinion to determine which is which.

recipients in the class that will multiply if abortion is stopped, who will use rather than contribute tax money, but let us leave this alone), and thus their preservation and support is a smart investment. This is a teleologistic response, and it could be contradicted if we can show a better way to produce tax payers, with less investments and less waiting time for the profit. This is an easy one. The world is full of hundreds of millions of people who are dying to immigrate to the U.S. We can choose to allow into the U.S. any number of people, any age group, any ethic group, any profession, and we have an endless supply of tax payers in each category. Especially good candidates are people from the East European ex-communist countries, where people are highly educated. So why invest in what we can get free of charge? Thus Crum's response is worthless, but at least he was being fair by giving a teleological response to a teleological claim.

As for the rest of the arguments, this tactic would not work for him, so he is forced to abandon fairness and hit below the belt. This he does by elevating the "conceptus' right to life" above women's rights, not only to autonomy but also to their mental and even physical health, and thus automatically pre-empting any conceivable pro-choice teleological argument. What puzzles me is [if this is really the case] why he even bothers to go into details, instead of dismissing all the arguments with one short sentence. I will now point out some additional specifics, relating to argument #2, #3, and #5.

Argument #2:

Here it is claimed that abortions decrease child abuse. Crum's response to that is that "abortion constitutes a greater (if I were he, I would have said 'the ultimate') child abuse." Well, only a professional dogmatist can say that aborting a fertilized egg or an embryo is a greater child abuse than the torturing of, say, one-year-old child.

Argument #4:

In this argument abortion in the case of risk to the life of the pregnant woman is discussed. Here Crum's ethics really goes wild when he proposes to give equal weight to the lives of the mother and of the conceptus. How dare he compare a living person having emotions, intelligence, education, life experience, social ties, and the many other characteristics that makes us human, with a piece of tissue, only potentially a human being (and who knows what kind) and currently living outside the real world, with only parasitical ties to its carrier who does not even want it? In this argument Crum does not even suggest giving a woman's life greater weight on accounts and on behalf of the babies she might have in the future if her life is saved, who also have a "right to life."

Argument #5:

Here Crum deals with the disputed right to abortion in the case of rape, a right that Crum denies, saying that "the unborn child is innocent of any crime," as though abortion is performed as a punishment to the conceptus[3] (and how can you punish an entity that does not know what punishment is?). Rather, as we all know, abortion is a medical procedure used to relieve a woman in despair of a part of her problem, where loss of the conceptus is but a side effect. Furthermore, Crum finds it more difficult to force pregnancy upon a raped woman than upon a woman who willingly engaged in sex knowing the risk involved. This sounds like he is implying that pregnancy is a punishment for whoever dares to express her (God given) sexuality, a crime she has to pay for by "serving time," nine months in jail of pregnancy with no possibility of parole.

In his conclusion to the chapter, Crum emphasizes the superiority of his ethics over the utilitarian arguments of the pro-choice, who are "forced to fight with one hand tied behind their back" due to their moral inferiority. This, of course, would only be true if they adopted his view that the conceptus is a full-fledged human being (and maybe not even then). However, the pro-choicers do not feel any obligation to endow the conceptus with such a status. For many of them it is only a result of accidental union of sperm and egg, which can also easily be achieved artificially by man, in-vitro, and which can be undone if the pregnancy threatens to infringe upon the woman's quality of life. Thus the pro-choicers fight with both

---

[3] As the innocence of the unborn is mentioned, then it must mean something; namely that if the unborn was not innocent abortion would or might be okay. That makes abortion a punishment of the unborn.

their hands free, feeling no moral inferiority towards the "pro-lifers."

Crum's Chapter III:
RIGHT TO LIFE VERSUS AUTONOMY

Crum defines the pro-choice concept of autonomy as the right of any individual to do as he or she pleases as long the action is not harmful to others. Phrased differently it implies that "you cannot legislate morality." Crum refutes the last statement pointing out that "all laws have moral component to them." As proof he asks us to name one action that (1) should be a serious crime and (2) is not immoral. Since he predicts that we will be unable to name such an action he concludes that we can and do legislate morality[4]. This analysis of the interrelation between morality and legislation is in line with the religious approach. *It views the state as an instrument to impose Judo-Christian morality upon the general populace, the same way Houmeini views the state as an instrument to impose Islam.* The secular approach, which is explained in my not yet published book entitled *Common Sense*, is as follows:

Yes, it is true that every action that is criminal (due to its being harmful to society at large or some of its members) is also immoral. This is so, since in order

---

[4] Crum's method of deduction is outrageously wrong. All that can be deduced here is that *serious crimes* ARE *immoral,* but not that *they are serious crimes* BECAUSE THEY ARE *immoral.* If we replace in (2) "immoral" by "a sin according to Islam" then using Crum's (incorrect) method of deduction we must (erroneously) conclude that we also legislate Islam.

to survive it makes sense for society to enact laws that protect members from harmful action of other members; and since it further makes sense to educate the members to avoid taking such harmful actions, not only from fear of reprisal or punishment, but also due to their recognition that they must accept restraints on themselves if they wish society to restrain others from harming them. Thus in order to minimize the number of policemen needed to enforce its laws, society conditions our consciences to police us. As we call the restraints dictated to us by our consciences as a result of conditioning by society "morality," it can be concluded that ***morality was invented by society, as it endorses as moral codes all laws it must enact for the protection of its members.*** Which means that what society is doing is ***not legislating morality,*** but exactly the other way around, ***"moralizing" legislation,*** that is, declaring as immoral anything that it deems necessary to make illegal, and in particular criminally illegal. We can call the part of morality comprising the collection of all such moral codes "Protective."

It turns out, however, that there are some so-called moral codes that do not fall into the category of Protective morality. Among those are, for instance, all codes pertaining to the regulation of sexual behavior: premarital sex, adultery, promiscuity, prostitution, homosexuality, oral sex, anal sex, etc. Many people will tell you that all of those acts are immoral. (In fact, many people would deem practically all pleasurable acts as immoral.) We can call this type of morality Non-Protective (or Religious Oriented, or Subjective, or Normative). Now, what is meant by "you can't legislate morality" is that *Society should not be entitled to legislate Non-Protective morality* (as opposed to its being *obligated* to legislate Protective morality). The abortion issue falls somewhere in between, depending on whether or not, or in what stages the conceptus deserves protection. We will deal with this problem in the comments to the next chapter. Before that, I wish to analyze the examples given by Crum to "legislation of morality."

Some of the examples brought up by Crum are: prostitution, suicide, selling oneself into slavery, driving on the wrong side of a highway, and shooting your neighbor. Now, the last two are obviously not victimless, so they constitute Protective morality and their prohibition is in order, in fact mandatory. Prostitution is indeed victimless and (not withstanding its immorality in the eyes of many) should not be outlawed any more than should any other consensual act of illicit sex (premarital, ex-marital, homosexual, etc). The only reason prostitution is singled out is because the victims of its outlawing (the prostitutes) are weak and lack political backing. Suicide is not victimless, it is murder that a person commits on oneself. To deal with this case we have to deal with the more comprehensive question of whether society, which is empowered to protect individuals from others, is also empowered to protect individuals from themselves. This is indeed a hard one. On one hand such intervention on the part of society contradicts the principle of autonomy by denying individuals the right to act freely. On the other hand it protects these individuals' autonomy from being destroyed altogether (by themselves), sometimes never to be used again. In order to solve this contradiction, we have to look upon autonomy both globally as well as locally. As we live in a dynamic world, our choices to a greater or lesser degree, depend on (changing) circumstances or moods; a choice one makes today may be different than the choice one makes tomorrow, perhaps because of a rough, sleepless night, or because of unkind treatment by another. That is how we make choice locally, at a particular moment. Now, if the choice is not substantially detrimental, and it is substantially reversible, then there is little justification for society to interfere. If however, the choice we make is damaging and irreversible, that is, we are cashing in on our local autonomy at the expense of our global autonomy (as a result of being in a disposition that makes us temporarily incapable of seeing the whole picture and making a rational judgment, or of controlling actions that are against our better judgement), then the element of protection (from self!) is strong enough for society to interfere. Now, suicide is one such action. It is totally irreversible. It is usually committed by people when they are psychologically low, and if they are given the chance, they will overcome their troubles and choose to stay alive. By preventing them from killing themselves society acts as a time delay mechanism and is, in fact, the protector of their global autonomy. By contrast, a decision to commit suicide may be rational, as is the case where a person is terminally ill and suffers pain. Here society has no right to interfere.

Slavery is another issue. It is more of an academic question than a pragmatic one, as I do not see long lines of people offering themselves as slaves. Indeed if the law permits a person to sell oneself into slavery for life, and the sale is enforceable, then we have an irreversible action that, by our rule, should be prohibited. Likewise, even if the slavery is temporary (say, a couple of months) but during its period the master may cause permanent damage to the slave, then again the action is detrimental and irreversible. If, however, the contract is temporary, and the slave is protected from undue bodily harm, the action should not be outlawed. Whether or not such a contract should be legally enforced is another matter. In this context we must remember that some forms of slavery are prevalent in our society. A contract between an employer and employee (say between movie production company and an actor), which prohibits the employee from working for another company, or a marriage contract, which prohibit the parties from engaging in intimate relations with others, and commits them to each other "for better or for worse," (for catholics, for life), are forms of slavery.

We can conclude that every intervention of society in an individual's action harmless to others is patronizing, and it can only be justified if the individual becomes tangibly or physically a victim of himself, as it is in the case of unjustified suicide. Some religious or feminist organization would justify the outlawing of prostitution by saying that the prostitutes are also victims of themselves. But they cannot show any *tangible* and *irreversible* damage caused to the prostitute as a result of her engaging in her chosen profession. Furthermore, the prostitute can justify her choice by using a philosophical argument that is just as strong and legitimate as that of the objectors, except that hers is non-normative, or outside the main stream (like this very intelligent college graduate prostitute in Amsterdam, who said to me: *"Business is business, love is bullshit, and money is a souvenir"*). Therefore, nobody has the right to steal the autonomy of the prostitute, just because they do not approve of her conduct, whether the disapproval comes from religious fundamentalists on grounds of the "immorality" of the act, or whether it comes from feminist organizations based on the premise that prostitution is exploitation of women by men. They all have to remember that the determination as to whether or not she is being immoral, as well as the determination as to whether or not she is being exploited is up to the lady. Whoever is not authorized to control feminine body parts by forcing women to bear children against their will also is not authorized to control feminine body parts by telling women under which circumstances, and in exchange for what, they are allowed to have sex. This is outright and uncalled for patronizing.

And look at how absurd and enslaving this infringement upon the woman's autonomy and her human dignity becomes. On one hand she is prohibited from using her feminine body parts to engage in an act that is rewarding to her (and her clients) and is harming no-one, and on the other hand she is forced to unwillingly submit her feminine body parts to the pro-lifers' use to satisfy their "high ethical" needs and breed their sacred fertilized eggs.

Crum's Chapter IV:
SCIENCE AND PERSONHOOD

Introduction and Definitions:

Unlike the previous one, this chapter for the most part is excellently written, and it seems like the author did his homework. Various definitions of personhood from post-birth to conception (why not go beyond that?) have been fairly presented and almost fairly discussed, in an effort to solve academically a pragmatic social problem. The search for consistency, however, becomes compulsive *ad absurdum*. For instance, the definition of Brody (in agreement with the assertion by Sass) is based on the belief that "the beginning of life should be normatively consistent with the ending of life." This requirement has no basis because the end of life is usually an instantaneous occurrence, and once death takes place, it is final. The creation of life is a process. It has no beginning in an absolute sense, and fertilization is just one particular stage in the process. We can say that for a particular person at a given time there are criteria to determine whether he or she is alive or dead, and here indeed death should be the negation of life. But to compulsively connect the dynamic process of creation of life with the instantaneous ending of life does not make sense. Indeed, when we consider the presence of brain waves as a criterion, we must realize that they are nothing but a symptom or indicator and do not represent a status. In the case of embryo, their presence might mean only that a certain area, namely the brain, starts developing particular cells (so what?); whereas, in the case of brain death, the absence of brain waves indicates that a particular individual who was a person in full sense (mobility, intelligence, communication, social ties, etc.), not only is no longer in that position, but will never be in this position again. So, the effort to define "the beginning of life" for the embryo by the same criterion as "the end of life" for a person is artificial and futile.

Crum finally reaches orgasm, when he presents the conception (fertilization) personhood. In order to make his bed soft, he uses as a mattress a quotation from Pearl Buck that supports his position that destruction of the fertilized egg is killing: "We are now what we were then, in every cell. . . ." What is being ignored here, is that the fertilized egg has parents, the unfertilized egg and the sperm, which uniquely determine its genetic code. Each of those is a half-gener and the combination of these half genes also "live in us in every cell." Crum does not tell us why their destruction is not killing. The fertilization personhood, by this approach (here, I quote former Surgeon General Everret Koop) is "to prevent a

Persons and Potential Persons

Believing he has been successful in proving scientifically the pre-eminence of the conception criterion for personhood, Crum states (page 44) that this findings "completely settle the argument of 'potential persons'" so that "it can no longer play havoc with the ethical and public policy decision-making process." Yes, Dr. Crum, indeed it is time to talk about the concept of "potential persons." Counter to what you seem to think, we are not as free here to select names that suit us for public relation purposes, as we were when we selected names for the opposing parties in the debate (pro-life and pro-choice). The terms "actual" and "potential" already have definite meaning in the English language, and there is a rational way to solve the mystery as to which one applies to the conceptus . To do this all is required of us is to decide whether the conceptus deserves protection — if it does at all — on account of *what it is* or on account of *what it might or would become*. If it is the former, then the conceptus is an actual person, whereas if it is the latter, it is only a potential person. To help us make this decision, let us suppose that at a certain stage, say three months into the pregnancy, the conceptus stops developing. It will continue to be alive in the womb but will remain at this stage of development forever, namely, for the rest of its carrier's life. The question before us now is whether ethics or the law should force the woman to remain pregnant for the rest of her life in order to preserve the life of a forever-three-month-old fetus.

I am sure some religious people would answer positively (they are even against destruction of unused fertilized eggs in the case of in-vitro fertilization). But as Crum speaks in the name of secular ethics, intellectual honesty must dictate that he answer negatively. In that case the argument about the potentially/actuality status of the conceptus is indeed settled: If the conceptus' life deserves protection it is not due to what it is, but due to what it would become, that is, the conceptus is but a *potential human being*, just as the sperm and the unfertilized egg are; except that it is at a more developed stage.

What, if any, protection, does this potential person deserve? Crum says that when we discriminate between the unborn and the born we practice a kind of racism, because our denial of personhood for the unborn parallels the denial of personhood for negroes. Well, so far as negroes are concerned, the question is settled, and there is no longer any public argument about their personhood. Hence, we can deal with the status of the unborn as a completely separate issue. The truth of the matter is that we are constantly practicing legitimized or condoned discrimination. The mere discrimination between people and other living things is "racism", or speciesism practiced by the human race against other species. In fact, we also discriminate among different species according to their location in the hierarchy of species. The dog is superior to the fly, which is superior to the amoeba. By law you can be punished for mistreating your dog, but not for mistreating a fly. A horrible, disgusting TV commercial by "Black Flag" tells us how disgusting these little creatures (roaches) are, and that "they deserve to die". During all these many years of the airing of this commercial none of the pro-lifers who demonstrate so vigorously and violently around abortion clinics ever protested against this anti-life commercial.

The discrimination between the species actually works in such a way that the closer a species or an animal is to the human race, the more consideration it gets. But now, if the superiority of man over animals is due to his spiritual attributes rather than to physical ones, and if the embryo, as is, is less similar to a human being than is a dog (the dog has feelings, understanding, ties, mobility, senses and can communicate on higher level than the embryo), it follows that if a living thing is to be protected for what it is, rather than of what it could or would become, then clearly the embryo deserves less protection than does the dog (which proves again, yet from another angle, why the unborn must be regarded only as a potential person!). If we are consistent in our thinking we must accept the reality that discrimination is indeed perpetrated against the conceptus to the same extent that is practiced against animals, and that the conceptus, for what it is, is biologically (and socially!) inferior to members of the human race. There is no shame in acknowledging it. It is true that it is emotionally disturbing to see a conceptus destroyed due to its similarity to us (and the pro-lifers do not hesitate to pull this string!), but by the same token,

I feel lousy when I have to kill a bug (as a landlord I am required by law to do this for my tenants in mass-murder proportions), or observe an animal killed for meat.

We must conclude that the conceptus is but a potential person, with potentiality increasing as the pregnancy progresses. We cannot mandate its protection for what it is, since in various stages it is biologically inferior, even to animals, but emotionally we "give it more points," so to speak , because of its expected final form as an equal to us.[5] One can look at a destroyed fetus and say: "This could have been another Einstein, or Mozart, or Roosevelt, or Darwin" (well, a pro-lifer probably would not wish for that one), and such a speculation can melt the hearts of many. But just as justifiably, I can look at my condom when it is thrown to the garbage after

---

[5] To shed more light on our approach, it would be interesting in this context to present analysis of the case of drug abuse or excessive drinking by pregnant women, which poses high risk to the health of their fetuses. Should such conduct be permitted? There is no doubt the pro-lifers would say no, since according to them the fetus is a person who is being harmed. What would a pro- choicer, like myself, say? Crum would probably predict that since the pro-choicers do not mandate the protection of the life of the unborn, obviously they should not mandate the protection of its health (a lesser right perhaps) either. He would be right, if the woman plans abortion. But if she decides to bear the child then my answer would be identical to the pro-lifer's, except that the reasoning is different. Since we now know that the unborn will become a child, then in fact she is harming not only a fetus (for which she should be absolved), but also a child, that (once born) has the right to be protected. Thus society has a duty on behalf of the child to stop the woman from perpetrating this harmful act. One has to note that society does not have to wait for the harmful consequences to actually take place in order to act, the same way society does not have to wait until after a murder is committed in order to stop the conspirators. We can say in this case that the woman is guilty of conspiracy to assault the health of a child upon its birth.

use, loaded with half a billion potential persons (sperm), and ask myself how many Einsteins and Mozarts and Lincolns and Darwins were just disposed of. Thus the same claims on behalf of the conceptus are also applicable to the sperm.

Pragmatic Personhood

We can approach the subject of personhood starting from the post-birth criterion, but look at it socially instead of biologically. We can look at the interest of society to protect its members not as a moral issue, but as a pragmatic one. We can imagine a contract between members of society prohibiting them from harming one another, and appointing the state to supervise it. A party to this contract would be anyone who can harm others but consents to be prohibited from doing so in exchange for his own protection. Theoretically, a newly born baby cannot be considered a party to this contract, not until he is able to understand the rule: "do no harm, and no harm will come unto you." This is the point were society is obligated to protect him, which is the social post-birth criterion for protection-deserving personhood. Since this point varies from person to person, and because it is very difficult to detect, we need some "security zone." Besides, since most babies have social ties to parents or other relatives, their protection from birth onwards is included in the protection of the interest of these adults. All of that makes any post-birth personhood impractical, thus leaving us no choice but to compromise and go back to personhood at birth, where we find ourselves in line with the general consensus. Considering graduality of the development of the fetus from before birth to birth it could make sense to extend protection even somewhat into pregnancy, letting it fade away towards some point in the last trimester — a more than fair compromise with the ethicists. Any protection at the expense of woman's autonomy beyond that is absolutely unjustified, because *unlike a Humeini Republic where religious dogma is the law of the land, the U.S. is a democracy where the imposition of religious mystical morality is prohibited by the Constitution and should be prohibited even when disguised as secular ethics.*

It may be very nice of us to strive toward pure, ultimate, sterile or germ-free ethics, but this will force us to become vegetarian, coexist with rodents (as their destruction would then be unethical), refrain from defending ourselves against violence (as the end does not justify the means), etc. We do live in a realistic world, and we must balance ethics or wishful ethics with reality. We may call the compromise "pragmatic ethics" (as opposed to "germ-free ethics", which is only wishful). We can at most pressure women not to abort at the end of the pregnancy, but the social cost (loss of autonomy for half of the populace) of the extreme ethics of the pro-life, which is not shared by the general populace, puts their ethical requirement outside the realm of pragmatic ethics, so that it cannot be imposed on the population at large. Crum claims that since the right to life is greater than the right to autonomy[6], then even if the unborn just "may be" a person, its right to life should supersede the woman's right to autonomy. This claim is obviously a fallacy. Neither the "right to life" nor the "right to autonomy" stands by itself. Each is only meaningful when attached to a subject. Suppose we agree that, for the same subject, the right to life is greater than the right to autonomy, and that for two equally graded subjects the right to life of one is greater than the right to autonomy of the other. But once we talk about subjects of different quality, the woman and the conceptus, one is definitely a person, whereas the other is at best a "may be" person (which can also be said of the sacred cow whose soul may be the incarnation of a human soul), then we are trying to compare *two unequal rights of two unequal subjects,* and we have no ethical means of doing that.

Thus it is not true that ethics dictates that the unborn should be given preference. Legally the woman has a right to autonomy. In fact, one can say that *if she has the fundamental right to bear children, she must also have the fundamental right not to bear them.* The conceptus "may be" has rights, but *until it is*

---

[6] We all are familiar with the saying "give me liberty or give me death", which puts the right to autonomy first. But this saying does not represent reality as it is inconsistent with our penal system which regards the death penalty as more severe than jail. Yet the slogan expresses the idea that liberty is an extremely important part of life, and the right to autonomy is almost as essential as the right to life.

proven it actually does have them[7] *he has nothing, as no ifs or maybes can serve as basis for legal conclusion that deprives others of their fundamental rights.* Hence the rights of the woman must be legally preserved and the speculation about the rights (or lack thereof) of the unborn should be left to the conscience of each and every woman. We can say, that while women have *rights*, concepti at best may have *privileges*, which may or may not be granted to them, *the guarantor being their carriers and not the state.*

In the context of public policy concerning abortion we must also touch on the question of federal funding of abortions. I resent both the Reagan and the Bush administrations for abusing their presidential power in order to impose on the general public policies dictated by extreme minorities who call themselves the "Moral Majority." I believe that the American people should decide for themselves where their tax money should go. As we know, when we file our income tax returns, we are asked whether or not we want $1 of our tax money to go to the presidential campaign. We should also be offered a choice of whether or not we want $1 of out tax money to fund abortions and I can bet my $1 that more dollars will be contributed to the funding of abortions than to the funding of the presidential campaign.

---

[7] This can never be proven because the "may be" does not stand for "something we do not know now and perhaps will find out at some future time," but rather for "what is forever undeterminable" as is the case regarding the humanness of sacred cows.